As One Door Closes

As One Door Closes

A Memoir about the Plane Crash of
Northwest Flight #255

Annie Weissman

Library of Congress Number: 2002094522
ISBN: Hardcover   1-4010-7508-8
                 Softcover   1-4010-7507-X

This book was printed in the United States of America.

To order additional copies of this book, contact:
Xlibris Corporation
1-888-795-4274
www.Xlibris.com
Orders@Xlibris.com
16298

For Emily and Elizabeth

I want to thank my family and friends for their unwavering support during the best of times and the worst of time.

Thank you to the young men in my life: Nick, Eric, and Max. For the sake of simplicity, I had to roll many friends into a few characters. Thank you to Linda Smith Pomeranz, Susan Bailyn, Carol Hebert, Susan Garvin, Elissa Rose, Veronica Marshall, Karen Eger, Marcy Figueroa-Stewart, Sharon Theisen, and Karlene Arnold.

I also want to thank all the teachers and members of critique groups I've been in throughout the years at the University of Iowa's Summer Writing Festival, the YMCA's Writer's Voice, the Hassayampa Writing Institute and the Sunday morning SCBWI group. It's taken a long time to refine this book.

Thanks especially to Mary Sojourner, for her insightful suggestions.

Dear Emily,

My life has shattered like a china teapot, never to be pieced together.

I was lying on the black leather recliner, watching "Sixty Minutes" when a message flashed across the bottom of the screen. I didn't see it soon enough to read it. Probably a storm alert.

Twenty minutes later another announcement scrolled at the bottom of the screen. "A Northwest Airlines plane crashed after take off from Detroit. The flight was due in Phoenix at 9:07 p.m."

I sat up straight in the chair, with my eyes locked on the television screen. Northwest flies all over the world. *The arrival time was just a coincidence . . .*

My life closed twice before its close;
 It yet remains to see
If Immortality unveil
 A third event to me.

So huge, so hopeless to conceive,
 As these that twice befell.
Parting is all we know of heaven,
 And all we need of hell.

 -Emily Dickinson

Annie, Emily and Elizabeth 1986

Annie's parents, Drs. Rae and Ben Weissman

CHAPTER 1

August 1986

"Hope" is the thing with feathers—
That perches in the soul—
And sings the tune without the word—
And never stops—at all—

-Emily Dickinson

The week before school started I took my daughters to my school library to help me get ready.

Twelve-year old Emily perched on my desk, cutting out lily pads, frogs, and toads for the bulletin board. Her porcelain face was flushed, bringing out the freckles on her nose and cheeks. Even air conditioning can't stop the August Phoenix heat. Still, not a hair on her auburn head was out of place. She looked immaculate in the outfit she'd bought at her grandmother's: white denim shorts, a pink polo shirt, and spotless white sneakers.

Six-year old Elizabeth sat on the carpet, occupying herself with paper, markers, scissors, and crayons. Her brown hair, cut bowl style, was sticky with sweat and curling up at the ends.

The intercom interrupted us in our work.

"Ms. Weissman, are you in your room?" asked the disembodied voice of the school secretary.

"Mommy," Elizabeth yelled. "You got a loud announcement!"

"I'm here," I said to the speaker box.

"I'm sending someone down with a delivery."

A few minutes later a delivery woman entered the room with a large vase of perfect ruby roses. I thanked her and smiled when I read the card.

"Are those for me, Mom?" Elizabeth chirped.

"They're for me, Elizabeth. Dan sent them. He's a man I met while you were away."

"Is he old or young?" Emily asked. "That guy you went out with last spring, Boring Bill, was too old!"

"Dan's about my age. How're the frogs and toads coming?"

"I've almost finished cutting them out, Mom. What's next?"

I surveyed the room. I had spent three days last week cleaning the shelves, chairs, and tables, and hanging posters of children's book illustrations, *Where the Wild things Are, George and Martha,* and *Ben's Trumpet,* over the wooden bookcases. The bright blue row boat I'd built was filled with blue, red, and yellow patchwork calico and jeans pillows I'd sewn during the summer.

"I think we need a break in a place with better air conditioning. Let's go to Pancho's."

We headed into the oppressive 113 degree heat, swelter as usual for Phoenix, and made it to the school office, where we washed up.

My spartan Toyota Tercel was an oven. Both girls climbed into the back seat.

"I can't do my safety belt, the metal part is too hot!" Elizabeth whimpered.

"Stop being such a brat," Emily said.

"It's okay, I'll drive carefully," I said.

After the car was parked, we hurried into the restaurant, luxuriating in the blizzard of cold air that met us at the door. It was early for lunch and there were few customers in the darkened restaurant. Its walls were decorated with colorful serapes and embroidered sombreros. The hostess smiled at us and led us to a booth.

"You got home so late last night we haven't had a chance to talk about your trip. How was New Jersey?" I said.

"Grandpa Ben didn't take us fishing. He read and rested," Emily said. "Nana Rae took us to the beach almost every day and I used Grandpa Ben's boogie board. One day we baked cakes and jelly tarts. Nana Rae took us to the Statue of Liberty, the Museum of Natural History, and the U.N., because Elizabeth hadn't been before. Aunt Evvy, Uncle Rami, and Melissa came for dinner three times. Melissa showed me how to French braid my hair and put on eye shadow. She's only two years older than me and she wears it to school!"

"Plus Grandpa Ben made a tape of me and him telling jokes," Elizabeth said. "I told knock-knock jokes. Grandpa Ben says I'm going to be a star! And they have new leather chairs in the TV room. Grandpa Ben calls them his "butter-soft" chairs. He and I fell asleep in them almost every day before dinner. But Grandpa Ben was tired all the time. He could hardly walk down to the ice cream store. We had to sit on a bench on the way home. How come he's so tired, Mommy?

"I don't know, Wizzie, I guess he wasn't feeling well,"

The waitress interrupted us long enough to take the orders for Elizabeth's quesadilla, Emily's chimichanga, and my chicken enchiladas.

"I really missed Mexican food!" Elizabeth said.

"It was so different in Ohio," Emily said. "Grandma took us to the mall and bought us fancy clothes to wear to lunch with her friends. Elizabeth and I got matching loafers and deck shoes. Elizabeth also got a pair of white patent leather shoes but Grandma got mad because Elizabeth got stains and scuffs on them."

"I had to stay in the corner for a long time for that," Elizabeth said. "Grandma bought me a party dress that twirls. Why didn't Nana Rae buy us clothes?"

"People have different ways of showing love, Elizabeth," I said. It was a great line for the kids because I didn't want to say what I really thought of Rob's parents. Thank God for short attention spans.

"I can't wait to see my friends. I'm going to call Rachel and Amanda when we get home," Emily said. "How many days do you want us to help you at school, Mom?"

"I need to go at least four more days, but you don't have to come."

"If it's okay with Amanda's mom, can I go over there tomorrow? Maybe Elizabeth can play with her brother."

"We'll call them today before we go out to dinner with Dan. Elizabeth giggled. Emily tried to keep a straight face.

"You must really like this guy, Mom. We never go to dinner with your dates."

"You are too smart, Emily. Dan is a 'big crush' as you would say."

Our lunch plates arrived, overflowing with sour cream, guacamole, and lettuce. We ate with relish and slurped the last of our sodas.

"Mom, can we stop at the gas station and get a huge soda for this afternoon?" Emily asked.

"You got it, babe," I replied.

*　　*　　*

The dinner with Dan and the girls was a cautious delight. Elizabeth lapped up the attention he showered on her. Emily was more aloof, rolling her eyes at his corny expressions, delivered in his slow drawl. But she winked at me when Dan put his arm around me.

*　　*　　*

The next weekend I met Dan's boys, Nick and Eric.

The noises in the bowling alley reverberated, reminding me of our busy school cafeteria. I held the heavy ball in my hand, took three steps and let it go, hoping for the best and winced as it went into the gutter for the fifth time. Nick and I were against Dan and Eric. The losers would treat to ice cream.

I loved watching Dan and his sons. They were natural athletes. Both boys were Norman Rockwell cute. Nick's red hair and Eric's almost white hair were cut in the same short preppie style as Dan's. They seemed like puppies, poking and pinching each other behind their dad's back.

Six-year old Eric found his ball, walked up to the line, and heaved it forward. Seven pins tumbled down. He ran to his father and they hugged. Eleven-year-old Nick took his turn, and knocked down all the pins.

"A strike!" he yelled. He ran and hugged me. I was taken by surprise but I hugged him back. The boys were supposed to be sullen and jealous with me, at least that's what Lisa, the teacher in the next classroom, had warned.

My fingers were stiff. I looked at the score sheet and was relieved to see we were almost done.

After the last ball was bowled, Dan added up the scores. "Annie and Nick won by fifteen points."

Nick hugged me and said, "I want a banana split with three kinds of ice cream and toppings."

"Dad, it wasn't fair!" said Eric. "If we play one more game, we'll beat them."

"We don't have time for another game," I said quickly. "It's eight-thirty and I want time to enjoy my ice cream before you have to go."

"Eight-thirty isn't late," snorted Nick. "We stay up as late as we want, watching television. We usually fall asleep on the couch."

I looked over at Dan who shrugged his shoulders as we headed out.

Mary Coyle's Ice Cream Parlor was a landmark in the Encanto neighborhood. Its pink and white striped wallpaper and pink leather booths were as sweet as its icy delights. Dan allowed Nick to order the biggest banana split on the menu. Everyone else ordered single scoop hot fudge sundaes, which were served with abundant hot fudge in little pitchers.

"Did you know my dad when my mom and dad were married?" Eric asked quietly.

I'm sure I flinched.

"No, I met him when you were back in Missouri with your mom and grandparents."

"My mom knew Buster, her boyfriend, when Mom and Dad were still living together." He dug into his sundae.

I looked down at my sundae, scraping the last of the hot fudge from the folds of the fluted glass. Dan was quiet.

For a while the only sound was spoons clinking on glass.

Nick ate valiantly but there were great globs of ice cream and toppings left. Dan took a spoon to it and finished it off.

"I'll walk you to the door," said Dan as we pulled into my driveway.

I turned to the back seat and said, "Good night Nick, good night Eric. I enjoyed meeting you." By the time I stepped out, Dan was next to me.

"They're cute and sweet," I said.

"Just like their dad," said Dan with his twinkling eyes smile as he walked me to my front door. He enfolded me in his arms and gave me a quick kiss. Loud smooching sounds came from the open windows of the car. I laughed, gave Dan an exaggerated puckered kiss, and went inside.

I watched from my plant-draped kitchen window as his car backed down the narrow driveway. When it was out of sight, I poured my decaffeinated tea, with lots of ice, and sat at the old pine kitchen table I had found at my neighbor's second hand store.

He likes my kids and I like his. It's too perfect.

I sipped my tea and started to cut out flannel board figures for a story I was preparing to tell.

Hard to believe I'd only known Dan three weeks.

* * *

CHAPTER 2

Wild Nights—Wild Nights!

Were I with thee

Wild Nights should be

Our Luxury

-Emily Dickinson

I had met Dan in a bar on a sweltering Phoenix summer night. I had gone to Carol and Terry's house for a gourmet feast and we decided to dance off the calories at an "oldies music" bar. It had a black and white tiled floor and flamingos everywhere.

At the end of the bar I saw a tall, strawberry haired man whose large frame appealed to me. I sucked in my stomach and squeezed through the crowd towards him. My heart pounded in my ears. I couldn't figure out why I was so nervous. It wasn't like it was the first time I'd asked a guy to dance. This was the 80's, not the 50's.

"Would you like to dance?" I asked.

He shrugged his shoulders.

"Sure," he grinned and led me through the bobbing, bouncing crush of dancers to a space just past the 1956 pink and black convertible where the DJ sat. Aretha Franklin's voice was belting out "Respect" as I let the beat enter my body and move my hips. My frosted hair swayed in sync. My partner barely moved. He looked like he wanted to be anywhere but the dance floor.

When the song ended, we moved to the edge of the crowd. I was sweaty but jazzed. That's what great r and b does to me.

"Can I buy you a drink?" he asked.

"I'd like a white wine spritzer but I'll pay it."

"Would you feel better if you paid for mine, too?"

I laughed. "No, just mine."

We got our drinks and found a quieter corner.

"I'm Annie," I said.

"I'm Dan. Do you often ask men to dance?"

"I wanted to meet you and didn't know how else to do it. Tell me about yourself."

"I don't usually go to bars," Dan said. "I was on my way back from checking on my house, watering the bushes, and taking in the mail. My wife and I separated in June. She and my two sons are in Missouri, visiting the grandparents."

"What happened to your marriage?"

"I'm not sure," Dan said. "One weekend we went to a golf tournament. I thought we had a great time. On Monday she told me to move out."

"Have you tried counseling?"

"We went a few times. My wife said she needed some time alone to figure things out. When I asked her how long it would take, she couldn't tell me whether it would be a month or a year.

Bag that! I don't get it. Everything was fine for fifteen years, then it's all wrong because I ran the show. Are you divorced?"

"Yes. My ex-husband is a lawyer in Phoenix. We were married for twelve years. I've been on my own for five. The best part of the marriage is my two daughters. What kind of work do you do?"

"I own a small business. What about you?"

"I'm a school librarian. I'm also taking courses for my principal certification. I thought I wanted to stay with kids and books forever but I've had two principals in a row that were sorry excuses. I figure I could do the job better, so I started taking classes at ASU."

We talked over the music and he asked me to dinner the next night. I wrote down my phone number and address on a damp cocktail napkin.

Sinatra's "Strangers in the Night" wove through the smoky air.

"How about another dance before we go?" Dan asked.

At first we danced a foot apart, but we were drawn together like magnets, with the electric current almost visible. His chubby cheeks felt like pillows on my head. His body fit mine. His hand on my back was firm but sensuous. My body juices bubbled. At the end of the song his lips softly brushed mine.

A hot August night wind nearly knocked us over as we left the cool air of the Golden Oldies Palace. We walked through the parking lot, detouring so I could admire his new car, a gray luxury edition of the Ford Taurus. After I had oohed and aahed, we strolled over to my car. He waited until I fastened my seat belt, locked the doors, and turned on the engine.

*   *   *

I saw Dan for the next three nights in a row. Then he asked me to go to Sedona with him the next weekend. I was nervous about putting my life in the hands of someone I'd only known a few days. I called my best friend, Susan, in California, and told her about Dan.

"Annie, infatuation overpowers common sense, I'm an expert on that. Do you trust him?"

"I feel cozy with him. It's just weird that we've gotten so close so soon. I have no idea where we're staying, whether in the same room or what. I'm too embarrassed to ask."

"I'm the last person on earth to say don't do anything impulsive. You're thirty-eight and you need some excitement. If you trust the guy, go for it! You need to get over your divorce scars. I can't imagine the life of a single mom. Speaking of mothers, mine is coming for a visit next month. She's staying for eight whole days."

"Susan, that's too long for you. Your mother's mouth works on you like rain on sugar. I'll call to remind you what a wonderful person you are. How are the illustrations coming for our book?"

"I just sent the packet off to Dr. Trejo yesterday. I used gouache in pastels and it took a long time to get the colors right. The illustrations are not realistic; they're whimsical. I hope you like them."

"I don't get an opinion. It's rare that I got any say at all. Publishers have their own artists. We were lucky that this is the company's first picture book and Trejo let me choose you to illustrate it."

"Well, I hope you like the drawings, Boo."

"I'm sure I will. I hope I like this weekend, too!"

*   *   *

The weekend was upon me. When I closed my over-full suitcase, an hour remained before Dan arrived. I shook my head, "I can't believe I'm doing this, I've only known him a week!" Another voice cajoled, "Go ahead, take a risk for once in your life."

I went into the living room and sat down on the love seat that faced the street. The picture window spanned most of the front wall. I picked up a P.D. James book and became so immersed in the story that I was startled when there was a knock on the window. Dan peered in at me. I jumped up and hurried to open the front door.

He put his arms around me and gave me a soft kiss on the mouth. The doubting voice in my head was hushed. "I'm ready to roll," I said when he released me.

Dan eased his six foot three inch body behind the wheel. I buckled up by the window and tried to relax, rubbing the gray velour seat that had the texture of a boy's buzz cut.

"There's some pop in the ice chest, along with ice and cups. Why don't you make us some drinks?"

My hands were shaking so much I almost spilled the soda.

"Here's to our weekend," he said while we touched cups.

I guzzled the Diet Coke and bubbles exploded down my throat. I choked. Dan laughed. I immediately felt better.

"We came in third place in the golf tournament," Dan said.

"I started out with a few good holes, but I beat it around on the back nine. The guys I play with are goofy, so we had a good time. We won gift certificates at the pro shop. Check this out."

He twisted his body so I could see the 'Mesa Country Club" insignia on the left side of his shirt.

"How often do you play golf?"

"Every day that ends in 'y'. I don't have to be in the office all day. I do a lot of the selling part of my job on the golf course."

We cruised in comfortable chat and silence up the highway. Dan was so easy to be with. I didn't feel I had to put on a certain look or attitude with him. I could just be myself, no extra frills or deception.

An hour and a half went by before I caught my first glimpse of the red rocks of Sedona. Their vermilion color, as always, took my breath away, though I'd see them many times. We passed Bell Rock, so perfectly formed that I always expected to hear bell tower chimes ringing. The crimson cliffs seemed to burn in contrast with the green of the few junipers dotting the jagged inclines. The black cloud shadows enhanced the bald, stark, purplish-scarlet of the mountains. The dirt was wet and dark red, life's blood flowing to the mountains. I opened my window and inhaled the junipers' perfume, loving this place with each breath. It seemed I was in my own enchanted land.

I walked around the suite at Los Abrigados, the resort Dan had selected. The living room had a humped-backed couch and an armoire with a television. The bedroom had a king size bed with a fluffy rust and gold geometric bedspread, another television, and a sink with a vanity in a corner. I had never stayed in such luxurious accommodations. I glanced again at the bed and found myself wondering whether Dan wore boxers or briefs. My face flushed as I imagined him in both.

"The couch pulls out to a bed," he said, "so there are two places to sleep. I told you there were no obligations attached to the trip. Let's get settled and head out for dinner."

The Owl was a rough wooden building that belied its more formal atmosphere, accented with white tablecloths, candles, and individual floral arrangements of daisies, sweet peas, and bachelor buttons. Dan ordered a Stoli and cranberry juice and I ordered my standard white wine spritzer, not too many calories, not too much booze.

He told me about his divorce.

"We're doing joint custody," he said.

"I hear that's how custody goes in divorces now."

His face tightened and he lowered his voice, "I don't care if Diana likes it or not. There's no way I'm giving up my kids. I'll probably do all the driving back and forth, but I'm going to see them anytime I want."

He perused his menu. I pretended to read mine. I wanted to feel his skin next to mine. I wished I'd packed the black satin nightgown. Better keep the conversation on safe topics, or I'd never make it through dinner. The waiter approached and we ordered.

"I've been divorced five years, since Elizabeth was a baby," I said. "Rob, my ex-husband, is not as committed in time to my kids as you are to yours. He's *finally* taking Emily and Elizabeth for the second and fourth weekends of the month, and a week or two in the summer."

"How long have they been gone?"

"They were with my parents for two weeks and now they're in Ohio for two weeks. I love the freedom of not having to set an example. I eat ice cream for breakfast, shop 'til I drop, and stay up late watching old movies. I can go out with my friends and not hassle for a babysitter. But I miss them terribly."

"I want to hear about your girls," he said.

"Elizabeth is such a rascal. On the first Mother's Day I was a single mom, Elizabeth was twenty-two months old. She locked herself in the bathroom. I didn't know what to do so I called a neighbor who's a police officer. He came right over, telling me we had to get her out immediately or she might hit her head on the toilet seat and drown. I didn't panic until he said that! He used a credit card and opened the door in two seconds. Elizabeth was in there, unrolling toilet paper, and having a fine time."

"My kids are rascals, too. Eric is more likely to get himself into trouble. He has allergies and I called him 'Snortin' Norton' until he decided it wasn't funny anymore."

As we ate, I felt Dan's gaze caress my breasts. I wanted to be back in the room in bed, past the awkwardness of undressing, just doing it.

"Do you want dessert?" Dan asked.

"Only you." Oh God! I couldn't believe I said that!

"I think we're done here," he said with a wide, warm smile.

As we left the restaurant, I welcomed the cool night air. My skin was tingling. When we got into the car, I sat in the middle of the front seat, surprising myself by putting my hand on his thigh.

"This is just a slice of heaven," he grinned.

*   *   *

Two days later, back in Phoenix, I rushed into Le Body's maroon and brass lobby and signed in as Carol's guest. I spotted her on a machine that looked like it would crush her. We've been friends since we met in a consciousness-raising group in 1973.

"I'll meet you in the pool," Carol yelled across the room, "I need to finish my workout."

I picked out an exercycle that was not reflected in a mirror and programmed it for eighteen minutes with slight inclines. I've faced it. I'm a Lasagna woman. My 170 pounds still curved like an hourglass on my five feet nine inches. I smiled to myself. Over the long weekend Dan said his ex-wife looked terrible because she had lost too much weight. He'd never know what points he had made with that remark.

I climbed off the bike and went through the door to the pool. It was blessedly empty. I jumped in and did four laps each of the breaststroke, freestyle, elementary back stroke, and side stroke. Carol joined me and we swam a few laps together.

We went back to the locker room and got ready for the steam room. My towel didn't fit all the way around my hips so I placed the overlapping of the towel to the side so only my thigh showed.

Carol put the towel down on the shelf and sat on it, nude. Her Barbie doll figure had withstood the ravages of time and her hair was still blonde, straight, long, and shiny. I loved her anyway.

"Tell me!" demanded Carol. "I want to know all the important details about your weekend with Dan in Sedona. Numero uno: the truth, where did you sleep?"

"Carol, how come you always boil everything down to sex?"

"So you did sleep with him! Was it any good?"

"It was the best weekend I can remember. I know it sounds trite, but we just clicked. I feel like I've known him forever. We talked, laughed, ate, and walked by Oak Creek Canyon with the red rocks towering overhead."

"If I had realized you were going to fall for the guy, I would have gotten a better look at him at the Golden Oldies. Can this really be you, the Queen of No Risks?"

"I don't feel like I'm taking risks; I feel secure. The sex was mixed with tenderness. There's comfort and, hmm, animal magnetism."

We were quiet for a minute.

"How are things for you, Carol?"

"Terry's great, just working too hard managing the shop. I sure married a good man. Zobi's coming back from Colorado for a visit so I can see for myself how she's doing. She's joined AA. I can't believe I have a seventeen-year old daughter who's an alcoholic! Patrick's doing okay. He's only thirteen, but he's beginning to show signs of rebellion. We're all going camping and fishing next week. Can I handle a family vacation? I don't know. Terry'd better help out."

"We need to talk about your fortieth birthday party," I said. "I'm still planning to have it at my house. What would you like?"

"I loved the party you gave for Lisa when we all dressed up like old ladies to make her look young. The cat costume party for Betty was fun, but I think I would like a cocktail party. I want to dress up."

We discussed the details until the door to the steam room opened and a woman with silver hair but no wrinkles on her face stepped in.

"I'm hot and ready for a shower," I said.

"Yeah, I'm getting hungry too. How about Mexican food?"

"I can almost taste a margarita. Let's get out of here, forget the makeup and hair."

"All right," agreed Carol, "but we'll have to sit in a dark corner."

*   *   *

CHAPTER 3

For every Bird a Nest

-Emily Dickinson

I surveyed the living room and dining room with a critical eye to see if everything was ready for Carol's birthday party. Navy blue cloths were smoothed over the kitchen and dining room tables, both now situated under the picture window in the living room. The giant glass shrimp cocktail server was stuffed with a medley of red, orange, and light green balls of fruit I had carved out of honeydew, cantaloupe, and watermelon. The tortilla rolls were prepared using Susan's step-by-step long distance directions: spread cream cheese on flour tortillas then paint a stripe of jalapeno jelly down the middle of each tortilla; roll each one up tightly; and slice. The rolls were displayed on their sides, looking like green and white pinwheels on the silver platters, leftovers from my first marriage.

I went back into the bedroom to look at myself in the full-length mirror behind the door. My eyes went straight to the neckline of the wrap around, magenta silk dress. I pinned the front so my bra wouldn't show, but cleavage did, just enough to feel daring and sexy but not too much to feel self conscious or cheap. I lifted my eyebrows, inhaled and exhaled deeply. It was okay.

Dan arrived first, followed by Carol and Terry.

"Good eats," he said as he sampled the tortilla rolls.

The guys fixed themselves some drinks and grazed on the food. Carol and I went into the bedroom for a private chat.

"Happy birthday! You look fabulous in that shade of orange!" I said. "Are you feeling young?"

"I feel young because Terry is fifty-four. I've got to tell you about our camping trip. Terry and I sat around, drank beer and philosophized. I think it's the most we've talked in months. We discovered we miss each other. I'm thinking about looking for a new job."

"But you've worked so hard to become an executive director!"

"I still want to be in charge but I'd like to find a smaller agency so I wouldn't have to put in so many hours. I want it all: good job, good marriage, good kids, good friends. Is that too much to ask?"

"It's what most women want and no one seems to have. Of course there are some flaws in the package. My job, too. Every year I forget how tired I get from lifting and shelving all those library books. And every year I hope the district will hire a clerk to do it."

"The schools in my neighborhood have clerks. Why don't you switch school districts?"

"I'm not a free agent. Another district won't give me credit for more than five years of experience. They don't hire anyone with the amount of education I have; it's too expensive. I would lose about $10,000 to go to a district with library clerks. Besides, I like working in South Phoenix. I'm needed. And it's a real neighborhood with all kinds of people."

The guests arrived in groups and tended to stay in clumps around the room. Dan stationed himself behind the bar and made drinks.

By eleven o'clock, people were dancing and singing along with the oldies radio station. It was just after one in the morning when the last people left.

Dan and I collected all the used glasses, plates, cans, and napkins. We emptied the ashtrays and washed the dishes. Dan took two large garbage bags out to the trash barrels in the alley.

"I need a shower!" he said. "It was tropical in here after everyone arrived. You need your air conditioner checked."

"It's just an old house. I replaced the gas powered air conditioning unit last year. The new electric one is much more efficient, but it still can't cool down the place with that many bodies when it's 98 degrees at ten o'clock at night. How about a shower together?"

*   *   *

The next morning Dan left to golf with his friends. I called Susan before heading out to the ASU law library to do a paper for my school law class.

"Carol's party was a big success," I said. "She still looks better than I've ever looked, young or old."

"Carol's body is her blessing and her curse," Susan said. "Those Playboy centerfold curves attract men like white on rice, but she's not very good at choosing one. Remember, she's on her third marriage."

"The first two were disasters," I agreed, "but Terry's a keeper. He didn't fit her notions of a good husband. He's retired navy, not a college graduate, and manages an auto repair shop. But I give her credit for looking for what she really needed: a good, steady, and loving man. I called to find out how the visit from your mom is going."

"I can talk, she's taking a shower. I'm surviving but she isn't even nice to Vanessa, which brings out my mother defenses.

My mother criticizes Vanessa constantly, bringing back all the hurt feelings of my childhood. My mother thinks the only person who does anything right is David. She must say ten times a day that I should thank God that he married undeserving me. It's hard to take."

"I remember when we would be at your house after school," I said, "eating clam dip on egg matzohs. As soon as your mother walked in the door, she would start in on you. 'That outfit looks terrible on you, Susan. It makes you look even fatter than you are.' It's pretty scary that she was a third grade teacher."

"Yeah, I wonder how many children she ruined with her sarcasm. I guess that's why I'm so paranoid about Vanessa's schooling."

"Remember Susan, you are a beautiful, sensitive, sweet, intelligent, generous, caring woman, a wonderful artist, my best friend, and an outstanding wife and mother."

"Thanks. How's your romance with Dan?"

"Hot and heavy. I see him almost every night. He comes over after dinner when Elizabeth is ready to go to bed and Emily is doing her homework. It's nice now that Emily is twelve and able to babysit for short periods of time. Dan and I go out for a walk and just laugh. He always has new jokes from the golf course. He's lightened up my life. I'm not so serious all the time. He often stays until three or four in the morning, but he leaves before the girls get up. Emily's at the age when dating has a new meaning because she knows more about sex. Elizabeth is easy. Dan plays with her, so she likes him."

"You've got two great kids."

"Does Vanessa like her preschool?"

"Yes, I'm glad I did the research to find the right one. The teacher is great and talks to me every day when I pick Vanessa up."

"Emily likes her teacher. All of her classes are accelerated, so she has to study for the first time since she started school. She has a lot of homework but she does it on her own. Elizabeth loves her first grade teacher. I think that little rascal can read, but she isn't letting anybody know. She still sleeps with her books. Her best friend goes to the after school care program, so she's happy."

"We miss you. Take it slow with Dan."

*   *   *

The next Monday afternoon I was in the library, waiting for Lisa to join me for our soda and gossip session.

She entered with a serious expression on her face. She handed me a Diet Coke and we popped the tops. We sat around the only adult height table in the room.

"It was a great day!" I said. "The kids enjoyed the flannel board story of 'Anansi the Spider' I told them."

"Shawn and Joey were absent," Lisa said. "I actually got to teach without interruptions. It makes you realize how much energy you're putting out for a few kids, and how much more you could be teaching the other students."

There was a short silence.

"Annie, as your friend," Lisa said, "I have to tell you my impression of Dan from the party. I know that you're in the 'swept away' stage but have you given any serious thought as to how different you are?"

My teeth clenched.

"He's a mucho macho male with 'sports' written all over his face," Lisa said. "I'll bet he hasn't read a book in the last twenty years! He's just shopping for someone to take care of his sons. You're the perfect mother, just look at how wonderful Elizabeth and Emily are. You've raised them with no help from Rob."

Lisa pressed on. "You're outgoing, he's withdrawn."

My throat got tight and tears built behind my eyes. Was I responding to her criticism of Dan or my own doubts?

"Annie," Lisa said gently, "you're just too nice for him.

He's looking for a wimpy wife and mother for his kids so he can continue to do whatever the hell he wants."

The tears rolled down my cheeks.

"I don't know why you don't want me to be happy with him," I said. "I see a side of him that you obviously don't. I won't choose between him and my friends."

"Annie, I am your friend, even when you make mistakes."

"He's not a mistake! He's the best thing that's happened to me in a long time. Are you jealous that I finally have a man? Or of the time I spend with him?"

"Whoa, let's not make this into a big thing," Lisa said.

"It's my choice to alternate between dating not at all and too much!"

We laughed, breaking the tension, and avoiding words that would have weakened the friendship.

"Just question the relationship a little. You're the best judge of what's right for you. Okay, I've got great gossip. I almost screamed when Tommy Edwards told me that his mom is going out with our principal!"

"The PTA president with the huge breasts? Mr. Harris isn't that stupid!"

"Could be!"

We had a good time speculating on the possibilities.

*   *   *

Emily slammed the back door and walked straight legged to the living room. She turned her body towards me but kept her face bowed to the floor.

"I got my social studies test back today. I got a "'D.'"

"Oh sweetie!" I said as I stood and hugged her. Emily's sobs were muffled in the folds of my denim jumper.

"I'm sorry," she moaned.

I petted Emily's smooth hair and sat down with her on the love seat.

"You don't have to apologize, Emily. I don't need you to get the best grades. You're the one who wants that. Did you study for the test?"

"Yes!"

"Did you figure out how to study smarter the next time?"

"Yeah."

"Then you realized something very important, how to learn from a mistake. If you can do that, you'll always be a success in life."

"You really aren't mad, Mom?"

"Not at all, sweetie. I've been anticipating this and I'm glad you finally got a bad grade. Now you know you don't have to be perfect."

Emily gave me a hug, wiped the tears from her face, and said, "I'm going to call Rachel, then do some homework."

"Okay, honey, remember I love you."

*   *   *

CHAPTER 4

Bring me the sunset in a cup.

-Emily Dickinson

It was still hot at four o'clock on a Friday afternoon in late September. Dan carried the last piece of luggage out to the car and squeezed it next to its many cousins in the trunk.

We set up a weekend for our children to meet. We were all going to a cabin in the tall pines of the White Mountains.

"There's a lake for fishing and boating," Dan said.

"Will you teach me how to fish, Dan?" asked Elizabeth.

"Sure will."

"You don't know how to fish?" Eric said. "I've been fishing since I was two years old. I've caught twenty-seven fish in my life. How much longer until we get there Dad?"

"We just started! It's a four hour drive. When we're halfway, we'll eat a picnic dinner at the bottom of the Salt River Canyon."

"Would you like me to tell you a story?" I asked.

"What kind of story?" asked Eric.

"My mom knows millions of stories and tells them to us all the time. I have tapes of them to play while I go to sleep," Elizabeth said. "Tell 'Molly Whuppie', Mom."

"Okay, this is my favorite story."

Once upon a time there was a man and a woman who had very

many children and hardly any money. They left the three youngest, who were girls, in the forest to fend for themselves. The two older girls were ordinary people, so they cried and they were afraid. The youngest was Molly Whuppie. She was bold and clever. She told her sisters to stop sniveling and start looking for a place to sleep.

They searched all that day. As night drew near, both of the sisters were faint from hunger, and even Molly Whuppie could hear her stomach grumble. Finally they saw a light in the distance. They crept closer and saw a huge house.

"What if a giant lives there?" whined one of the sisters.

"I don't care," said Molly Whuppie. "I'm hungry!"

She went up to the door and knocked. A woman answered the door.

"Please," said Molly Whuppie, "my sisters and I need some dinner and a place to stay."

"It's dinner you'd be!" said the woman. "My husband is a double-faced giant who eats children broiled on toast! When he came home, he would have you as a treat."

Molly Whuppie thought and thought and thought.

"Well, if he isn't home now, may we come in and have something to eat? We'll leave right away."

The woman had three daughters of her own, just Molly Whuppie and her sisters' ages. She took pity and let them in.

While Molly Whuppie and her sisters were eating bread and cheese around the fireplace, IN WALKED THE GIANT!

"Who's that eating my food?" roared the giant.

"It's just some poor little girlies, please don't hurt them."

Now this was a double-faced giant. He could be very kind with one of his faces, and very mean with the other. He decided to be kind. He allowed Molly Whuppie and her sisters to spend the night. He even wove them chains of straw to match the chains of gold his own daughters wore.

When it was time to go to sleep, all six girls slept in one bed. Everyone went right to sleep, except Molly Whuppie. She stayed up and thought and thought and thought. Then she took the straw chains from her own and her sisters' necks and put them on the giant's daughters' necks, exchanging them for the gold chains. Then she stayed up to see if she was right.

And she was! That double-faced giant came in but it was so dark he couldn't see a thing. He felt around for the straw chains, dragged his own daughters out to the cooking pot.

"Wake up!" Molly Whuppie told her sisters. "We have to go right now, before the giant realizes his mistake!"

They ran out of the house and into the forest. They walked all night long, looking for another place to stay. Finally, as the sun came up, they saw a castle.

"What if another giant lives there?" whined one of the sisters.

"I don't care," said Molly Whuppie, "I'm tired and I need a place to sleep."

The castle was surrounded by a moat. They saw no bridge until they looked carefully and noticed a bridge made of a single hair, naturally called The Bridge of the Single Hair.

Molly Whuppie balanced her way across the bridge and into the castle. There she found a jolly king with three sons.

It turned out that the giant Molly Whuppie had tricked had been terrorizing the countryside. The king gave a feast in Molly Whuppie's honor.

During the feast, the king motioned Molly Whuppie aside.

"Molly Whuppie, you are a very clever girl, but you could be cleverer still. If you will bring me the sword from over the giant's bed, I'll let your older sister marry the oldest prince."

Molly Whuppie thought and thought and thought. She knew that the sword held some of the giant's evil power, and it would be good to get it away from him. She also knew that the prince and her sister loved each other and would like to be married. It would be a dangerous task, but she decided she would do it!

That night she crept away from the castle and ran to the giant's house. She didn't knock at the door. She slipped in the back way, and hid under his bed.

By and by the giant came home, ate his supper, and went to sleep.

Molly Whuppie crept out from under the bed. She crept up the covers to the head of his bed. She saw the sword on the wall.

She carefully took it from the wall, but when she jumped to the floor, the sword rattled in its scabbard and woke up the giant!

She ran and he ran and they ran and ran and ran until they came to the Bridge of the Single Hair. Molly Whuppie held that sword over her head, and balanced her way across. The giant could not. Both of his faces were red with anger.

"Woe unto you, Molly Whuppie! Never you dare to come again!"

Molly Whuppie answered, "Twice yet, giant, will I dare to come again."

She went into the castle.

A few weeks later, Molly Whuppie's older sister and the oldest prince were married. During the weeding feast, the king motioned Molly Whuppie aside.

"Molly Whuppie, you are a very clever girl, but you could be cleverer still. If you will bring me the purse from under the giant's pillow, I'll let your other sister marry my middle son."

Molly Whuppie thought and thought and thought. She knew that the purse held some of the giant's evil power, and it would be good to get it away from him. She also knew that the prince and her sister loved each other and would like to be married. It would be a more dangerous task, but she decided she would do it!

That night she crept away from the castle and ran to the giant's house. She slipped in the back way, and hid under his bed.

By and by the giant came home, ate his supper, and went to sleep.

Molly Whuppie crept out from under the bed. She crept up the covers to the top of his bed. She saw the purse sticking out from beneath the pillow. She carefully tugged, but a double-faced giant has a very heavy head. She tugged and tugged until the purse came free, but some of its coins clattered to the floor and woke up the giant!

She ran and he ran and they ran and ran and ran until they came to the Bridge of the Single Hair. Molly Whuppie held that purse out in front of her, and balanced her way across. The giant could not. Both of his mouths were foaming with anger.

"Woe unto you, Molly Whuppie! Never you dare to come again!"

Molly Whuppie answered, "Once yet, giant, will I dare to come again."

She went into the castle.

A few weeks later, Molly Whuppie's sister and the middle prince were married. During the wedding feast, the king motioned Molly Whuppie aside.

"Molly Whuppie, you are a very clever girl, but you could be cleverer still. If you will bring me the gold ring from the giant's finger, I'll let you marry my youngest son, and rule the land."

Molly Whuppie thought and thought and thought. She knew that the ring held the last vestiges of the giant's evil power, and it would be good to get it away from him. She also knew she liked the prince. In fact they loved each other, and would like to be married. It would be the most dangerous task, but she really wanted to rule the land, so she decided she would do it!

That night she crept away from the castle and ran to the giant's house. She slipped in the back way, and hid under his bed.

By and by the giant came home, ate his supper, and went to bed. He snored very loudly.

Molly Whuppie crept out from under the bed. She crept up the covers, onto the giant's arm, and up to his hand.

The giant closed his hand around her. He had just been pretending to sleep with one of his faces!

"Now I've got you, Molly Whuppie. What would you do to me if I'd been as mean to you as you've been to me?"

Molly Whuppie thought and thought and thought.

"Well, Giant, I'd get a big sack. In it I'd put you, a dog, a cat, needle and thread, and a pair of scissors. I'd hang the sack on the fireplace. Then I'd go out into the woods, find the biggest tree, cut it down, bring it back, and beat you with it."

The giant got evil grins on both of his faces.

"That's exactly what I'm going to do to you, Molly Whuppie!"

The giant got a large sack and put Molly Whuppie in it with a dog, a cat, needle and thread, and scissors. Then he hung it up on the mantle while he went out to the forest to find a big tree.

As soon as he left, Molly Whuppie started to laugh. She laughed and laughed.

"What are you laughing at?" asked the giant's wife.

"Oh, it's too funny to describe!" yelled Molly Whuppie and she laughed some more.

"Let me see!" insisted the woman.

"All right," said Molly Whuppie. She cut a hole in the sack with the scissors. She took with her the needle and thread, then hoisted the woman into the sack. Molly Whuppie sewed up the hole in the sack. Just as she was finishing, she heard the giant coming. Molly Whuppie hid under the table.

The giant came in, took off his gold ring and put it on the table, then proceeded to beat the sack.

The giant's wife cried out to him, but he couldn't hear her since the dog and cat were being hit and they barked and meowed loudly.

Molly Whuppie did not want the woman to be hurt, for she had been kind. Molly Whuppie crept out from under the table and grabbed the ring. Out of all four corners of his eyes, the giant saw her.

She ran and he ran and they ran and ran and ran until they came to the Bridge of the Single Hair. Molly Whuppie held that ring around her waist, and balanced her way across. The giant could not. Tears were streaming out of all four of his eyes.

"Woe unto you, Molly Whuppie! Never you dare to come again!"

Molly Whuppie answered, "I won't!"

She went into the castle, she married the youngest prince, and she ruled the land happily ever after.

"Tell us another!" said Eric as soon as I had finished.

"Sure," I said. I told "Why Dogs Hate Cats," and "Tikki Tikki Tembo" until my voice was hoarse.

"We'll buy a blank tape and I'll record stories this weekend, Eric."

"Did you bring a tape recorder?" Nick asked.

"Elizabeth doesn't go anywhere without it," Emily said.

Later we drove in the dark through the White Mountains in northeastern Arizona. We finally found Pinetop and the nest of cabins. As soon as the children got out of the car, they yelled for sweatshirts. The temperature was 55 degrees, 45 degrees cooler than when we left Phoenix.

We explored our weekend home, using the flashlight from Dan's car to find the light switches. Dan hustled everyone back to the car to unload the mountain of suitcases and food. I hadn't realized he'd gone to the grocery store before he came by my house. Many of the sacks from the grocery store had chips and cookies showing on top. But he took the responsibility, I thought.

The cabin had a kitchen with a formica and steel table and chairs, a living room with a fireplace and old plaid furniture, a full bathroom and two bedrooms, each with a set of bunk beds and one with a double bed. The girls and I took the bigger room, Dan's boys took the other. Dan decided to sleep on the convertible couch in the living room. It was late enough to put all the children to bed. Emily, being the oldest, was allowed to keep the light on and read in bed, serenaded by the soft voice from Elizabeth's tape player.

Dan made a fire in the living room fireplace, then relaxed on the couch. I joined him, snuggling into my place under his left arm.

"The lake is in front of the porch," Dan said. "It's too dark to see it tonight."

"I didn't realize you'd been here before," I snipped, my jealousy aroused.

"Diana and I brought the boys here several times. This is the best cabin because we can hear the kids even when they go exploring."

Dan leaned over and gave me a long, wet kiss. "There's no one else I'd rather be with than you."

How did he always manage to say the right thing? I went to check on Emily and Elizabeth. Both were asleep.

When I came back into the living room, Dan was making the couch into a bed. He took off his clothes, hung his pants and shirt on a chair, and got under the covers.

"Aren't you going to join me?" he asked.

"I'm not comfortable sleeping with you in front the children."

"Oh, you can stay with me a while, then sleep in the bedroom with them."

I imagined his body under the sheets and found the vision seductive. I quickly took off my clothes and got into the bed shivering. We made love quietly, then I slipped into the room with my daughters.

The next morning, Nick woke up early. He jumped on Dan and

they wrestled, waking all of us. Nick and Eric gave Dan and me good morning hugs before Dan shooed them into the bathroom for showers. All of the choices of breakfast cereal were sugar coated, to the delight of Elizabeth and Emily.

After breakfast we got out the fishing gear and headed for the dock. The tall pines whispered in the breeze. The crisp air reminded me of New Jersey autumn mornings. The small lake was surrounded by high grass, pines, and bushes that were reflected in the still water. The cloudless blue sky went on forever. I'd forgotten what mountains were like. Maybe I'd stayed in the desert too long.

Eric and Nick took salmon eggs from the tackle box, baited their hooks, and started casting. Dan showed Elizabeth and Emily how to bait and cast. He didn't get impatient when Elizabeth asked him to fix her hook for the fourth time. No one got a bite.

I sat on a cream colored boulder under the shade of an oak tree whose leaves were already yellow. I was feeling easy, ostensibly reading a Chaim Potok book I'd picked up at the used bookstore. A fly kept finding me irresistible. Its buzzing was the only sound in the peaceful setting.

Eric went back to the cabin and came out with a can of Pepsi.

"Mom!" Elizabeth yelled, "Eric is drinking a Pepsi in the morning!" She put her hands on her hips and scolded, "Put the soda back, Eric. You're not allowed to do that!"

"I am too allowed to drink Pepsi in the morning. My Dad does it!"

I looked at Dan. He shrugged his shoulders and smiled.

"Elizabeth," I said, thinking fast for a solution, "every parent has different rules. Dan allows Nick and Eric to drink soda in the morning. I don't allow any sweets until after lunch. You and Emily need to follow my rules."

"Oh Mom! That's not fair."

"Fair or not, that's the way it's going to be."

Dan took Eric and Elizabeth in a row boat to see if the fish were biting in another part of the lake. I looked up when I heard shouting.

The boat wasn't far from shore. Elizabeth was bending over the side and Dan was telling her to sit down. The end of her fishing pole was bent and Eric was screaming, "She's got a big one!"

Elizabeth leaned over further. The boat tipped and she fell out. I leaped to my feet and ran to the edge of the lake that was closest to the boat. Dan called to Elizabeth to come to the boat. She couldn't swim because she wouldn't let go of the pole. Dan jumped into the lake and stood up. The water was up to his waist. He scooped up Elizabeth and her pole and deposited them on the shore and said, "You can't go in the boat if you won't listen to what I say."

I gathered my crying child up in my arms. "Are you hurt?"

"No!" screamed Elizabeth, "I lost a big fish with whiskers!"

I hugged her and chuckled. "You are such a rascal! It's a good thing I brought extra clothes."

Late that evening, when the children were asleep, Dan and I were in the midst of what he called "groping," when he lifted my chin with his hand so we were looking into each others' eyes.

"I won't say this often. I'm not that kind of person. Annie, I love you."

I breathed deeply and said with a cracking voice, "I love you, too."

That weekend Dan did all the cooking; I did the dishes. On Sunday afternoon we all pitched in to straighten and clean up the cabin. I noted that Dan was willing to show Elizabeth the affection that her own father didn't or couldn't. Elizabeth and Eric played make believe.

The situation reminded me of the "Brady Bunch". Could real life be this simple?

* * *

CHAPTER 5

'Tis customary as we part
A trinket—to confer—
It helps to stimulate the faith
When lovers be afar—

-Emily Dickinson

The next Friday Dan picked me up at school and we drove toward Pinetop. We ate dinner at a root beer place on the way out of town.

When we got back in the car, he said, "Open up the glove compartment. I bought another dessert for you."

I found the small square package wrapped in shiny white paper with a silver bow on it. Dan turned on the dome light of the car while I undid the outer layer carefully. Inside was a jewelry box. After I opened it, I flung it in the air, managing to catch the box before it fell to the floor. I inspected the ring inside more carefully. It was a thick gold band with a diamond sticking up in a Tiffany setting.

"What does this mean?"

"What do you mean, 'what does this mean?' That's a diamond ring! I'm asking you to marry me."

I was truly speechless for one of the few times in my life. On long walks in the evenings we had been playing the talk game, "when we get married." I thought of it as daydreaming an event far in the future. Two heavy weights were vibrating inside my stomach.

"Does your silence mean 'no'?" Dan asked.

"I wasn't expecting anything so soon. I've been enjoying falling in love. I like where we are now."

"Annie, I'm a guy who likes to be married. I don't like to be alone. I hate being single. I hate eating breakfast by myself. I hate throwing out the bread because one person can't eat a whole loaf before it gets moldy. I hate going back to my apartment at three o'clock in the morning because you think you're fooling Emily that we're not in bed. She's brilliant, for God's sake. She probably figured it out the first time she met me. I want to marry you."

"This is too soon for me. We still have a lot to talk about. We're different religions. How do our children figure in a marriage? You've never met my parents and I haven't met yours.

You haven't seen me screaming and grumpy, scouring my house for a hidden chocolate bar."

"Just try on the ring."

The ring went on but the style made my finger look like a hot dog decked out in a tight napkin ring.

"Why don't you wear it this weekend, try on the idea, and we'll talk about everything you want to discuss. On Sunday afternoon you can decide whether to wear it or return it."

"Okay, I'll do that."

Chocolate-covered words dripped from Dan's tongue that weekend. I thought about marriage when I was supposed to be studying School Law. He was watching a football game he'd bet on. We talked while we ate at a fancy restaurant, while we strolled around a lake, and while we shopped at a craft fair where I introduced him to the idea of buying Christmas presents during the summer.

We agreed to celebrate all the Jewish and Christian holidays. I readily agreed to have Nick and Eric live with us if their mother gave up custody. He explained the terms of his divorce, which would be final in December. He finally agreed to separate bank accounts. Rob had taken all our cash the summer we separated and I took Emily and Elizabeth to San Francisco. I came back to no money and no paycheck for a month. Unconditional trust would not be there for a second marriage.

By Sunday the only subject unresolved was names. At a pizza place on the way back to Phoenix, Dan ate and I sipped on iced tea. When I am in the middle of a Big Life Decision, I can't eat. In times of ordinary stress, I eat chocolate.

"I won't change my name," I said. "I took Rob's name and six months after I was married, I was sorry I had. I took my maiden name back after my divorce and intend to have it until I the day I die. It's who I am."

"I would much rather you went by my name, but I can see that you can't be persuaded. How about if I say fine to you keeping your name, and you say 'yes' to being engaged?"

During the weekend, the weights in my stomach had been replaced by butterflies. Getting engaged after knowing a man less than two months was such an impetuous thing to do, so unlike me. I'm the kind of person who always returns the grocery cart to the designated area. The timing didn't agree with my notion of how long I should date before getting engaged, but I knew Rob for four years and that hadn't lasted forever.

Dan didn't fit the image I had of a mate. I loved books, he only read the sports pages. He liked things in his jello, I liked it only plain and red. He liked shoot 'em up movies, I preferred musicals and romantic comedies. But he placed a high priority on children and family and I felt safe and happy with him. We also had the best and most often sex I'd ever known. Why not? To hell with convention and what others would think!

"You've got a deal," I said, amazing myself at my courage to do what I wanted.

"Hot damn!" he said. "I've landed my best fish!"

*   *   *

Later that afternoon, I sat in the love seat in my living room, chewing on my lower lip and waiting for Emily and Elizabeth to return home from their weekend with Rob. His red LeBaron convertible finally turned into the driveway. The girls got out and waved goodbye.

I rushed to open the door.

"Welcome back," I said hugging and kissing them. "Did you have a good weekend?"

"I got to go to Dad's office on Saturday and do my homework while he went through some files," Emily reported. "Elizabeth had to stay at Loretta's house because the last time she came to the office she made a mess and Daddy couldn't work."

"Loretta's house was fun, Mom," Elizabeth said. "We made cookies for Daddy and I helped her plant lettuce and radishes in her fall garden."

"I'm glad you had a good time."

I took a deep breath, then pursed and unpursed my lips.

"Dan asked me to marry him."

"Will we still be able to see Daddy?" Elizabeth asked.

"Of course, Wizzie," I said. "Dan will be your stepfather, but Daddy will always be your daddy. You'll see him the same amount as you see him now."

"Will Eric come and live here?" Elizabeth asked.

"Not right away, but it could happen in the future. How do you feel about me marrying Dan, Emily?"

"It's fine if that's what you want, Mom. Don't you think he should move in now so we can try it out before you get married?"

I was taken aback. "I thought that might be awkward for you, Emily. I know that twelve is a difficult age. None of your friends' parents are divorced and I thought it would be embarrassing for you if Dan was living here before we got married."

"What difference does it make? He stays here all the time anyway."

So she knew.

"I'll talk to Dan about it. You two are the most important people in the world to me. I told Dan that you would always come first. I'm not asking your permission to marry him, I just want to know how you feel about it."

"I like Dan. He's fun. Can I be in the wedding?" Elizabeth asked.

"Of course."

"If you're happy Mom, it's okay with me," Emily said. "When are you going to get married?"

"We're thinking about sometime in the early spring."

"Okay. Will you test me on my Latin vocabulary words now?"

"Sure, sweetie, how about a Mom sandwich first?" I stood up as Emily put her arms around me on one side and Elizabeth on the other side.

When both kids were in bed, I rushed to the phone to call Susan and Carol to tell them the news. Then I sat down and wrote a letter to my parents, pitching four drafts before I was satisfied.

*   *   *

I waited every night for my parents to call in response to the letter about my engagement to Dan. When a week went by and I hadn't heard from them, I projected criticism and rehearsed a speech before I dialed their number.

"We were very surprised about your engagement," my mother said. "How well do you know this man? Are you sure you want to move this fast?"

"Mom, I can't tell you why, but I'm sure it's right. I don't believe that time is the most important factor. I knew Rob for four years before we got married. We still got divorced. I met Dan at the beginning of August and I've seen him almost every day since then. We're planning the wedding for March. You'd better start looking for material for a knockout dress."

"Things here got more complicated this week."

"What's happened? What's the matter?"

"Dad hasn't been feeling well since last summer. He's been going in for tests and seeing specialists. We didn't want to say anything until there was something to report. He went to see an oncologist at Mt. Sinai yesterday. He's been diagnosed with lymphoma cancer."

"Oh my God!"

"He'll go to the hospital off and on to get therapy. The doctor will be sending orders to the local hospital for some of the medicine but we'll have to go to New York for special treatments and check ups and progress reports."

"How's Dad taking it?"

"Well, he's upset. He's never been sick. He hates not being in charge."

"Is he up? May I speak with him?"

"Sure, I'll put him on the phone. Ben, Annie wants to talk to you."

"Hiya baby, how're you doing?" my father asked.

"I'm fine, Pops. The question is, how are you?"

"I heard Mom tell you the news. I'm just trying to take one day at a time. They treated me well at the hospital until they realized the Dr. was PhD, not MD. The young doctors started to call me 'Ben'. I got sore and called them by their first names. Behind their backs I called them 'the three little boys from school.'"

"I'm glad you've still got your sense of humor. I want you to meet Dan, Daddy. I'll talk to him about going to New York over winter vacation. Take care of yourself. I love you Daddy."

"I love you too, baby."

*　　*　　*

All four kids ran from the car and exploded into the costume store. I hurried behind them to restore order.

"Remember why we're here. You may each pick out a costume for Halloween. Dan and I are going to rent costumes for the party."

"I gotta see this!" Nick said. "My dad is going to wear a costume?"

We all perused the photographs on the wall, displaying all the possibilities.

"You could both be crayons," Elizabeth suggested.

"How about Robin Hood and Maid Marian?" asked Emily.

Dan looked at the picture she was pointing to.

"No tights!" Dan said. "That's where I draw the line."

"What about gorillas?" said Eric.

"Too hot!" I said.

"How about golfers?" asked Nick.

"No, it has to be something that's not our ordinary life," I said.

"How about Raggedy Ann and Andy?" I suggested.

Dan closely inspected the photograph.

"Yeah, that's fine," Dan said. "Will you do the paperwork while I help the kids pick stuff for their costumes?"

"Sure, but I want to see the kids' accessories, too"

Eric chose a skeleton outfit, with a black body and white bones outlined so they mirrored the inside of his body. He wanted the skull mask with the bones and blood. Nick picked a satin cape and vampire teeth. I told him I'd put white face makeup with black around the eyes and mouth. Elizabeth chose a buckskin shirt and vest and a sheriff's star. Emily said she was too old to trick or treat, so she didn't need a costume.

"Are we going to the party, too?" asked Nick.

"No, it's only for adults," Emily said. "Mom always plans her Halloween party for when we're at my Dad's house. But she takes lots of pictures. All her friends dress up so weird. Last year Lisa and a friend came as Dolly Parton Siamese twins!"

At the Halloween party, Dan was convivial. Costumes usually allow people to shed their shyness and inhibitions. However, Lisa gave him a wide berth.

Carol and Terry were great as Mr. Spock and a female of his species. The best was probably the school psychologist who came wearing a Freudian slip.

*   *   *

The next week was a busy one in the library. I was grateful for the quiet after a noisy group of kindergartners left. I had stirred them up by having them act out *Where the Wild Things Are.*

I was shelving the mountain of books that threatened to topple off the book truck, when Paco, an eighth grader, came in. He was handsome and preppie in the Ralph Lauren polo shirt and jeans he was wearing, hand-me-downs from Carol's son. His black hair was combed straight back and accentuated his large brown eyes. Paco had caught my attention when he was in the fourth grade and I'd been guiding his reading, and him, ever since. I made sure he was placed in the program for gifted kids.

Last year, when he was in danger of failing, I made a deal with him. If he was behind in his assignments, he would have to stay at my house to complete his work. When I called his mother to suggest the plan, she readily agreed without asking for my address or phone number.

Paco fingered a feather and pinecone turkey a second grader had given me that day. He pulled the strings of a wooden Pilgrim jumping jack toy from the harvest display. Finally he came over to my desk.

His head was bent and he talked to the floor. "I haven't finished my poetry notebook. It's due tomorrow."

"How much have you done?"

He looked up and said, "I've picked out the poems and copied most of them neatly. I still have to write two poems. I don't have a folder so I haven't designed the cover. The cover is worth twenty points."

"I have School Law at ASU tonight but you can work at the back of the class. How about if we swing by your place at four o'clock, pick up some clothes for tomorrow, and tell your mom you'll be with me tonight? Then we'll stop at the store and get you a folder. You can write your own poems in here after school. If you need any help, let me know."

"Okay," he said. "I'll be back after my last period class."

I was still shelving books when Paco returned. He sat down at a library table, opened his notebook to an empty page, and put the eraser part of his pencil in his mouth. After a few minutes, he began to write. He worked quietly until it was time to go.

We could hear the yelling before they got Paco's apartment. He said, "I'll be right back."

Through the open door I could see Paco's mother, short and stocky, with a permanent scowl on her face, sitting on the couch and drinking a can of beer. Paco darted into the bedroom he shared with his two brothers.

"You God damned mother fucker!" his mother screamed at his retreating body. "You never do anything right! You were supposed to clean up this morning!"

My eyes went to the kitchen. The sink was overflowing with several days worth of dirty dishes. Bugs were nibbling the scraps of food that were everywhere on the counters and the floor. I swallowed the retort, "Clean it yourself!"

"Is it all right if Paco stays at my house tonight? He has a big poetry project he needs to finish," I said in as polite a manner as I could muster.

"Yeah, yeah, fine, keep him out of my sight."

I had stopped trying to understand Paco's mother. She was unlike most of the mothers of the Hispanic students. They were protective, concerned, and proud of their children. She was none of these. Paco came out of the bedroom, ran across the living room saying, "See you tomorrow" to his mother and out the front door. I followed him to my car, wishing I could take a magic wand and change his mother into someone who appreciated him.

Paco selected a folder at the drug store. He went with me to pick up Elizabeth at Cactus Club, the after school child care. When we arrived at my house, Emily was doing her homework. Paco joined her at the dining room table and borrowed her markers to work on the cover for his project.

"Time to make dinner, and you can help me, Elizabeth. Tonight I'm taking Paco to my School Law class, but I'll be home by 10 o'clock. Lisa will stay with you."

"Mom, I'm old enough to babysit Elizabeth for the whole evening," Emily said.

"You probably are," I said, "but I have to get used to the idea."

After dinner, Emily and Paco cleared the table and loaded the dishwasher while I got myself together for my class. I was almost finished with the course work for my principal certification.

Lisa arrived to babysit Elizabeth and Emily.

"I've got to get going," I said. "Elizabeth, go to bed without any whining. Emily, you can play backgammon with Lisa but be in bed by 9:30. Bye bye, I love you," I said as I kissed them. "Let's go, Paco."

He picked up his folder and notebook and followed me out to the car.

I spoke to the professor before class. He agreed to allow Paco to work in the back of the room. During the lecture, I stole glimpses of Paco while he wrote poetry. On the way home he asked me insightful questions about Brown v. the Board of Education of Topeka, the topic of the lecture. *This boy has such potential, I thought. Maybe he'll be a lawyer.*

*　　*　　*

I was annoyed with my parents. They never called anymore. Since I moved to Phoenix, almost twenty years ago, they called every Sunday at eight in the evening. Now I had to call them and wring information about my father's condition.

The voice on the other end was so weak; I thought I'd dialed the wrong number. "Daddy?"

"Hiya baby."

"I almost didn't recognize your voice."

"I'm feeling weak. The chemotherapy makes me nauseous so they give me more pills for that. The doctor says it's normal to feel bad. How are Emily and Elizabeth?"

"They're fine, and doing well at school. Emily's band teacher asked her to play the alto sax for the jazz band. We didn't have to rent it because the school had an extra one. He's very impressed with how quickly she's picked it up. She's still taking flute lessons and playing in the regular band. She's going to play at the wedding. Elizabeth is still into jokes. She also has taken up ballet at a parks and recreation program. Daddy, Dan and I want to visit you over Christmas vacation. Will you feel up to it?"

"I don't know, it's hard to predict. Maybe you should stay with your sister and just drive over and visit us for a day."

My father had never suggested I stay anywhere but with him.

"Sure, I'll arrange it with Evvy and Mom. Take care of yourself, Pops."

I put down the phone slowly. *My father was a strong man, a towering figure. Who was the sickly guy on the phone?*

*   *   *

Dear Daddy,

I'm so sorry that you will not be able to come to our wedding. It won't be the same without you here to walk me down the aisle. We'll take lots of pictures for you.

I thought I'd write a letter instead of calling because a letter you can reread whenever you're feeling up to it.

I love you, Pops.

I wanted to tell you of some of my favorite memories. Do you remember taking me fishing when I was about eight years old? You rented a rowboat on Lake Hopatcong. It was just the two of us. I caught six fish and you caught one. I remember thinking I was a wonderful fisher. You never pointed out that you did all the baiting of the hooks, untangling of the lines, and rowing. I can still see us on the lake, fishing poles in the water, talking. I do not remember a single subject on which we conversed, but the memory has the fuzzy edges of love.

When I was in third grade, you came to school and told the story of the "The Toothless Rabbit." All the kids were spellbound.

Sometimes the best part of my day was bedtime, when you told me "The Seven Legged Frog Who Needed Shoes" and "Sinbad the Forgetful Sailor," or read me a Shakespearean play. I thought it was a coincidence when you took me to see "Macbeth" right after you finished reading it to me. You instilled in me a love of Shakespeare at age nine. You read it with such relish, playing all the parts and explaining what was necessary for Joe and me. You didn't ruin it by asking comprehension questions and giving tests.

The car pool to Sunday School was fun when you drove. Poor Walter never knew of your perfect impersonation of his nasal voice!

When you read the poems I wrote my junior year of college and gave constructive criticism, it hurt. But it taught me that all writing had to be revised. "That's good!" from your lips caused an explosion of pride and happiness that ran from my head to my heart.

I love you Pops, now and forever.

Love,
Annie

*   *   *

CHAPTER 6

Love's stricken "why"
Is all that love can speak—
Built of but just a syllable
The hugest hearts that break

-Emily Dickinson

Dan, the girls, and I spent Thanksgiving with Carol and her family. Eric and Nick were with their mother for the holiday. We picked them up in the evening so we could get an early start the next morning for Nogales, a border town in southern Arizona.

Nick got up first, before the alarm clock, and roused everyone to an even earlier start than expected. We ate breakfast at Picacho Peak, halfway between Phoenix and Tucson. I had recorded an hour's worth of stories to distract the children from the boring scenery. We sang songs, told jokes, and arrived in Nogales a jolly crew.

We checked into a basic American hotel. Right away the kids wanted to know the sleeping arrangements.

"Nick and I will take one bed," Dan said. "Emily and Annie will sleep in the other. Eric and Elizabeth get to play 'camping' using sleeping bags on the floor."

Eric and Elizabeth looked at each other, then at us. I couldn't tell if they were going to complain until they both showed those rascal smiles.

"We'll have to be careful of bears," Eric said. "My dad sounds like one at night."

"And we'll have to use a flashlight to find the bathroom," giggled Elizabeth.

"Okay, let's unload the car and go to Mexico for lunch!" I said.

"I don't want to go to Mexico," Nick said.

"Why?" asked Emily.

"I've never been to another country," he answered.

"We've been to Mexico, camping, loads of times," Elizabeth bragged. "We go to Rocky Point all the time and sleep out on Sandy Beach."

"What if they don't let us come back to Arizona?" Eric asked.

Dan chanted

"If 'ifs' and 'buts'
were candy and nuts
we'd all have a Merry Christmas."

"What?" asked Eric.

"There's no problem at this border crossing," I said. "Many people cross every day to work and to shop."

Eric took Dan's right hand while Nick grabbed Dan's left hand. They didn't let go until we had crossed the border and were seated at "La Caverna," a restaurant built in a cave where Pancho Villa hid.

Nick turned up his nose at the taco he was served.

"The cheese is white and crumbly. It's supposed to be orange and in even pieces!"

"I know it looks different, Nick, but try it," I urged.

He warily picked up the taco and took an infinitesimal bite. Then he took a regular-sized bite.

"It's . . . okay," he said. "It's not a real taco, but it tastes good."

"Maybe it IS a real taco, Nick," I replied, "and the ones you eat at Taco Bell are the imitation."

At lunch I explained bartering and we told the children they were each allotted five dollars to buy themselves a present. We would decide together on gifts for their grandparents.

As we walked over to the main shopping district, the children were awe struck by the tiny children selling chicklets and begging for money.

"They aren't out here for spending money," I said. "They are very poor and need the money to live."

"We should give them our five dollars," Emily said.

I looked at her and smiled at her goodness.

"How would you spread it among all these children and the ones that will be on the next block? Poverty in Mexico can't be solved by five dollars, though it's generous of you to suggest it. How about if we give dimes and nickels to each of the children we see? And you can still have your five dollars to shop."

"Can I have a dime for those two boys over there?" Elizabeth said, pointing to two boys, just a bit younger than she.

"Yes," Dan said as he found a dime in his pocket. "I hope you brought a lot of change," he said to me.

Initially I did most of the talking, since I was the only one among us who spoke Spanish. The vendors understood enough English so when the kids caught on to the system they bargained for themselves.

I took a picture of the kids posed by a burro painted like a zebra. When I told the kids that they should drink bottled soda while in Mexico, not milk or water, due to differences in processing, they cheered.

We also shopped for Christmas tree ornaments. When Dan had moved in the week before, we discussed having a Christmas tree. My ex-husband always had a tree but took all the ornaments with him when he left. Dan's wife got all his ornaments in their divorce settlement. Emily and Elizabeth were excited about having a Christmas tree in our home again. We hadn't had one since I separated from their dad. Elizabeth had only been a year old then. Part of the shopping mission in Nogales was to buy ornaments. The kids helped us pick out painted tin angels, woven straw bells, and carved wooden Santas.

We shopped, ate at a fancy restaurant above a furniture store, and returned without incident to the American side to sleep in our hotel. The next day we finished our shopping and drank margaritas while the kids drank Cokes and Seven-Ups, marveling at the small bottles.

On the trip home the following day, we stopped at a picnic area for lunch. Dan made sandwiches from the cooler. I took pictures of the kids showing off their purchases: Emily had a braided bead bracelet, Elizabeth demonstrated her kitten watch that opened, Eric spread out red dominoes from a wooden box, and Nick held up his black elephant carved from stone. A family of shoppers.

Emily and Nick pose in Nogales, Mexico

Eric and Elizabeth clown around while making wreaths

*   *   *

A few weeks later, the girls and I were home when the phone rang. Emily dove to get it first on the extension in her room. When I picked it up in the kitchen I realized Emily and Carol were already having a conversation.

"Carol, do you know how to make latkes, you know, potato pancakes?"

"I sure do. What's up?" Carol asked.

"Mom's going to make them from a mix for our Hanukkah party."

"Emily, I think the world of your mother, but cooking is not her specialty. I'll make the latkes."

"Thanks," said Emily, "I'll get Mom on the phone."

I soundlessly hung up the phone and waited for Emily to tell me to pick it up.

"Annie," Carol said. "I was thinking over your invitation to the Hanukkah party. Since I'm bringing my whole family, including my mom and dad, I'll also bring my food processor and make the latkes. I'd love to do it."

"Sure," I managed through the knot in my throat. It's not everyday I got the opportunity to see my daughter and my best friend manipulating me.

"How was the visit to meet Dan's parents?" asked Carol.

"Just fine. They're nice people, so kind and hospitable. They don't have the same southern drawl as Dan. His mother is from Michigan and his dad was born in Kansas. Dan's drawl must come from growing up in southern Missouri, where Springfield is.

"Do you think his parents accepted you?" Carol asked.

"His sweet mother told me that I'm the type of person she had hoped Dan would marry. I met his brother and sister-in-law and their three year old girl. Everyone was friendly. They're all coming out for the wedding, even his eighty year old grandmother."

"I'm glad something went well. Things have hit the fan at work. In the good column is the $125,000 grant my agency received. I spent a lot of time coming up with the proposal and writing the grant, so that felt great. On the down side, one of my staff members is bad mouthing me again to a Board member. The problem is that I don't know who the creep is. I'm going to have to be very careful about what I do and say at work."

"I don't know how you handle the politics of being an executive director. That's the good thing about working at a school. It's more fun if I get along with the other teachers and the principal, but I can always just close the door to my library and ignore the politics. I hear Elizabeth calling me for her bedtime story. I'll talk to you soon."

*　　*　　*

Dan and I visited New Jersey the week after Christmas while our children were busy visiting their "other parents." We stayed at my sister's house. Even though I had warned Dan that my sister NEVER cooked, he was still stunned to open the refrigerator and find nothing but Diet Coke. We went to visit my parents the second day of our trip.

The rain melted the light dusting of snow that had fallen during the night. Dan and I hurried to the rented Chevrolet to avoid getting wet. The naked trees, the dark sky, and the rain fit my brooding mood. I was scared and worried about seeing my father and anxious about whether my parents would like Dan. He wasn't intellectual, he wasn't Jewish, and he wasn't a Yankee. I prayed my parents would get past that criteria. I also hoped Dan would make an effort to talk more.

The ride took two hours, with a lot of cursing from Dan about New Jersey drivers. As we pulled into the cul de sac, I pointed out the house into which my parents had moved when my dad retired from teaching political science at Rutgers.

My mom, a stooped woman with jet black hair and a whole face smile, opened the storm door, hugged and kissed me, and welcomed us inside. I sniffed Mom's cologne, Evening in Paris, always a harbinger of comfort.

She led us to the living room where everything looked the same: the rust, gold, and brown floral couch; the glass coffee table that my nephew had bumped his head on when crawling under it as a toddler; and the framed prints from my parents' trip to Italy.

I stopped when I saw a man in my father's wing chair. The shock came when I realized that the bald old man was my father! Gone was the thick silver and black wavy hair of which he was so proud. Gone were the bushy eyebrows with which he would fiddle when deep in thought. Gone were the full face and the potbelly.

His Lake Tahoe blue eyes had a mist covering their sparkle. The skinny old man raised himself carefully and slowly from the chair. I ran over and hugged him.

"Good to see you, pie face," he said.

"I've missed you, Daddy," I said as I released him and watched him sit down in the same ponderous manner. "This is Dan."

Dan walked over to the chair, shook hands and said, "It's a pleasure to meet you, sir."

"Just call me Ben."

"And call me Rae," my mother said. "Please sit down on the couch. Did you have a nice trip?"

"I would not describe the ride as 'nice'. Driving in New Jersey certainly is an experience I will remember for a long time," Dan said. "The drivers act like they've never heard of a turn signal and get points for how many cars they cut off. Now I understand why Annie drives the way she does."

"I guess we're so used to it, we don't notice any more," my mother said.

"How are you feeling, Pops?" I asked.

"I'm okay. The weeks after I take the chemotherapy are the worst. As soon as I start feeling good, it's time for more chemotherapy. I have to drink so much water it's a miracle I haven't been swept down a drain as I walk across the street. I put toothpicks in a jar for each glass I drink or I forget how many I've had during the day."

My father spoke in a voice that had half its usual timbre and vitality. I noticed that instead of using his hands to gesture, he kept them in his lap.

"Annie tells me you've got a business, Dan."

"I sell a service to car dealers that they furnish free to new car owners. We fix or tow new cars that have any kind of trouble on the road."

"Like AAA?"

"Yes, like their emergency road service, except the car owner doesn't pay for it. I do some of my selling on the golf course. I'm a good golfer and customers want to play with me, especially in their member-guest country club tournaments."

"Do you have a degree in business?"

"Yes sir, I was a sales and marketing major at the Southwest Missouri State University. I started out in Kansas City with a major corporation and was transferred to Phoenix. I got tired of the big company garbage, so I started my own business."

I took my mother's hand as we went into the kitchen to attend to lunch.

"Mom, Daddy looks terrible! Isn't the chemotherapy working?"

"The doctor said it wasn't working as well as she had expected, so they're trying alternate drugs. I forget how different he looks if you haven't seen him for a while. What would Dan like to drink with lunch? I bought some beer."

"He isn't a beer drinker. He'd probably like milk if you have it."

"No one will drink the beer here. I'll save it for Rami. Your sister's family still comes to dinner here every Sunday. Rami likes the verbal sparring with your father on politics. It's good for your father to have someone to challenge him. Everybody else is accommodating because he's sick; they won't get into an intellectual argument with him. He misses that. Let's call them to the table.

In honor of Dan's visit, the dining room table was set with the silver and gray trimmed china and the matching silver edged crystal. The tablecloth looked like an explosion of daisies, roses, asters, and mums. The cloth napkins were the color of the magenta roses on the tablecloth. The drapes of the picture window were open to show the back yard and at least a dozen bird feeders.

"Why all the bird feeders, Mom?"

"We enjoy watching the birds. I'm surprised at how many have stayed for the winter. We can sit for hours in the mornings with our binoculars watching and identifying them. We also have a few pesky squirrels with whom your father has been matching wits, trying to keep them out of the birds' food."

As we ate a tasty lunch of split pea soup and Chinese chicken salad, my mother filled me in on the news of the relatives, including, births, graduations, marriages, and divorces.

"I'm tired, I'm going to lie down in the bedroom," my father said as soon as we finished lunch.

"We need to get going anyway," I said. "We don't want to get stuck in the rush hour."

I hugged and kissed my father, incredulous at his bony grasp.

Dan stood up and shook his hand. "It's been a pleasure to meet you, sir."

"I'm counting on you to take good care of my Annie."

My father turned and shuffled down the hallway. His leather slippers made a thwapping sound.

We got back in the car. The rain had stopped so we drove to a nearby beach. It was deserted, not even someone giving a dog exercise.

I asked, "So how did you like them?"

"Your mother is sweet," Dan said. "It was a little hard to understand everything she said because she talked so fast. Your father is very sick. While you were in the kitchen with your mother, he grilled me. I should have brought my bank statement to show him I'm solvent."

"Oh God, I'm sorry!"

"It's okay, he just wanted to make sure I could take care of you."

"He's never accepted my independence, or my career, and now is not the time to argue with him. My mother told me they can't come to the wedding. Daddy isn't well enough to travel. Maybe we should postpone the wedding until he feels better."

Dan drew me close to him, putting his arms around me, and holding me firmly.

"He isn't going to get better, Annie."

"You don't know that! You're not a doctor!"

A picture of my father shuffling down the hallway came into my head and I knew Dan was right. He held me while I cried.

The drive back to my sister's house was long, with lots of traffic and too much time for me to think about how frail my father was.

*   *   *

When we went into New York City the next day, Dan was aghast at the filth, the prostitutes, the hard core porn movies in Times Square, and the bustle of the city.

We explored the American Museum of Natural History's dinosaur bones and the wild animal dioramas.

We took a taxi, always an adventure, to Tavern on the Green for lunch. The sky darkened and all the tiny white lights that outlined the bare tree limbs became visible through the restaurants window, surrounding us in a fairy realm. As I scraped up the last of my chocolate dessert, snowflakes began falling. On our walk over to 60th Street, the flakes stuck in our hair and on our coats. I was in a Cary Grant-Greta Garbo movie.

We went to FAO Schwartz and purchased toys for our kids that they would love but didn't need.

Dan kept finding pay phones to call his secretary. On the bus ride back to my sister's house in New Jersey, he told me that his business had been dealt a huge blow because a tow truck company had chosen not to renegotiate their contract. The tow truck company was going to become his competitor.

"There's no way I can compete with them," he said. His eyes had lost their teasing twinkle. "Their costs are much lower than mine. They'll probably 'borrow' my marketing tools. I'm fucked."

It was a somber ride. I had no business acumen to share with him.

*　　*　　*

When we got back to Phoenix, his business fell apart. He closed it at the end of January. He paid the creditors but didn't have money left for a new business.

*　　*　　*

A few weeks later a teacher at school couldn't use her airline ticket so I bought it cheaply and winged my way to San Francisco to meet Susan for a weekend getaway.

We browsed in the "special occasion" section in Macy's Department

Store in Union Square. Susan picked a pink suit off the rack and we headed for the fitting room. Although the ensemble fit, it was overpowering on Susan's small frame. We both shook our heads. Susan put on her own clothes.

"I needed this weekend and fun with you," I said, "even though we haven't found you a dress for my wedding,"

"I'm sure I'll find something in L.A. You've given me an idea of the style and plenty of choices in color," Susan said. "Tell me about your dress."

"Carol and I went to Azteca, the biggest bridal shop in Phoenix. I was going to buy a tea length dress, but fell in love with a long one with a train." I pantomimed as I described the gown. "It shows some chest but it's not scandalous. I do have to wear a special strapless bra that's down to my waist. The dress is fitted in the waist and has a hoop slip to puff out the skirt. The hat sits jauntily on my head. It reminds me of a nineteenth century English lady's fancy riding outfit from the front cover of a Delderfield novel. I guess I missed not wearing a long gown the first time I got married. When I look at the pictures of the mini dresses for my first wedding, I laugh."

"Do you remember that I cut the green velvet wrong and had barely enough material to make my dress? I had to put the flowers in front of my crotch so as not to embarrass myself. We were so young!"

"Yeah, I wouldn't want to be twenty-one again. I have no regrets."

"I hope you know what you're doing with this marriage. It seems so fast. And now Dan's unemployed. Maybe you should wait until he gets a job."

"I'm marrying him forever, not for the next few months. Dan has always worked hard. I have no doubt he'll continue. He needs my support now, not doubts. Susan, this marriage feels right."

"Okay," she said. "Do we have time to get a hot fudge sundae before we go to the airport?"

"There's always time for hot fudge."

We took the escalator to the basement floor of Macy's and walked to the food section. The ice cream concession wasn't crowded. We ordered the same sundaes we ate in high school: hot fudge with chocolate chip ice cream, no nuts or cherry and just a little whipped cream.

"There were no problems when Dan moved in. It's easier on me because he pays for half of the expenses. My life is just working out perfectly, Susan. I'm finishing up my classes to be a principal this semester. Our book is being published. I'm marrying a great guy. All four children are doing well. Everything is ideal."

My bubbles of joy suddenly broke with a vision on my bald father.

"I take it back, my life is not perfect. My father looked terrible when we saw him last month. He's lost all of his glorious hair. He still directs the conversations, but he doesn't give the all-encompassing lectures he used to. My parents can't come to the wedding. My mother feels she'll be there in spirit because she's sewing the dresses for Emily and Elizabeth."

We finished our sundaes in silence, knowing that we would always be the perfect eating partners and best friends.

*　　*　　*

Dan went to Mexico on a week-long fishing trip with his golf buddies. Why wasn't he busy looking for a job? The closure of his business shook his self esteem and stole the teasing twinkle from his eyes. He still gave me the money for his half of the monthly bills. How much savings did he have before I'd have to support us all? How could I do that on a school librarian's salary when I'd just taken out a loan from the credit union for half the wedding expenses and for Emily's bat mitzvah celebration.

The next week Dan followed up a newspaper ad for a salesman and was employed immediately by a roofing company.

"Do you know anything about roofs?" I asked. He sure wasn't handy around the house.

"No, but I know sales," he replied. "I only have to learn the product."

He didn't make much money at first, but he got a draw on future commissions. I finally relaxed when he sold three roofs in one day.

His new boss took us out dinner at the Salt Cellar. I didn't like the guy as soon as I saw him. He was tall and held himself in an intimidating stance. His thinning hair was slicked back. His smile was fake. I immediately nicknamed him "Slimebucket."

He insisted we order the two pound lobsters, even as I protested that I couldn't eat that much. He drank five martinis before dinner was served. He tried to shmooze me and looked quizzical when I didn't respond to his charms. A song from "My Fair Lady" popped into my head. Professor Higgins sings it after the triumph at the ball, describing Professor Carpathy (and Dan's new boss) perfectly. "He oiled his way around the floor."

I hoped socializing with the Slimebucket would not be part of Dan's new job.

March 15, 1987

Dear Daddy,

Elizabeth drove me wild with knock-knock jokes tonight. She certainly is a chip off your old block. I remember when your friend Merrill would come over on Sunday mornings and the two of you would do a vaudeville marathon. We'd sit around the kitchen table, eating bagels, cream cheese, lox, and white fish that Mom had brought in from the deli. You guys would keep us laughing for hours.

Do you remember your guitar phase? You bought an acoustic one to start with, but quickly added an electronic one that you hooked up to our super stereo in the basement. We could hear "Down in the Valley" all over the house.

I'll be finishing my principal's certification this semester. Several professors have asked me to consider getting an EdD and doing research with them. Don't get excited about this possibility because I heard enough about university politics at home to know they want to use me. I don't need the advanced degree unless I want to be a superintendent or want to teach full time at ASU. First I want to see if I can get an administrative job and like it before I concentrate that amount of time and energy.

I wish you were going to walk me down the aisle at my wedding next month. I'll be thinking of you as I walk alone.

Get better already!

Love,

Annie

CHAPTER 7

Oh the Earth was *made* for lovers, for damsel, and hopeless
  swain,

For sighing, and gentle whispering, and unity made of twain.

-Emily Dickinson

Time fast-forwarded to the weekend of our wedding.

I met Susan and her husband, David, at the airport. David carried two overstuffed garment bags and Susan had a large tote bag.

"Do you have more luggage?" I asked.

"Does the Mississippi River have water?" David snorted. "I think Susan packed every outfit she owns."

"I wasn't sure what I'd need," Susan said.

David arranged the hatchback trunk of my small car to accommodate the suitcases, carefully laying the garment bags on top. Susan and I sat in the front bucket seats and heard his sigh as he climbed in the back seat.

"What's the schedule?" Susan asked.

"Tonight Dan, his brother Steve who just arrived, Nick, Eric, and Paco are trying on their tuxedos to make sure they fit.

Emily and Elizabeth are waiting at the house to see you. I thought we'd eat some Mexican food at Mi Patio then we'd drive you to your hotel."

"Fantastic! I've been dreaming about a chicken Patio Taco with tomatillo sauce," Susan said.

As we headed west, I was awed by a Phoenix sunset: pink and navy blue clouds behind palm trees.

As we pulled into my driveway, Emily and Elizabeth ran from the house. When Susan stepped out of the car, she was smothered with hugs and kisses.

"Everybody squeeze in the car, I'm starved!"

Mi Patio, a restaurant built on the site of a defunct gas station on the corner of Osborn and Seventh Avenue, had pink stucco walls inside and out. The waiter recognized Emily, Elizabeth, and me immediately, and led us to a table.

"How about a pitcher of margaritas?" he asked.

"Perfecto!" I said, "Emily and Elizabeth, do you want strawberry daiquiris?"

"Sure."

"And two frozen strawberry daiquiris without any liquor. And a cheese crisp with strips of green chilies."

Susan turned to Elizabeth and said, "What have you been doing?"

"I haven't gotten my name on the board for talking this whole school year. I've read forty-four books for the reading club."

"And what about you, Emily?" Susan asked.

"School's fine. Some of the girls are being weird, but I stay out of it. I stopped being good friends with the popular kids and hang around now with the band kids. Rachel's my best friend. She plays the flute and is in my Hebrew and gifted classes. She knows how to be a friend, like you and mom. She has curly hair like yours, too. Our favorite subject is Latin."

"Remember how we used to work together after school on our Latin homework?" Susan said to me. "We had our 'ponies' to help us translate Caesar and *The Aeneid*."

"It does warm the cockles of my heart that Emily enjoys Latin," I said.

After we ordered our meals, I tuned out of the conversation and scrutinized my best friend. Susan's body had changed from medium to trim in the last four years. She was an aerobics devotee and worked hard to keep her short body petite. Her curly red hair was cut to form a halo of ringlets around her face. How diligently we had tried to straighten our hair in high school! Susan's face had few wrinkles, even though we were both thirty-nine. David put his arm around the back of Susan's chair. Their marriage of seven years seemed to be comfortable and happy despite a tortuous courtship. It was hard to believe that Susan, the career woman, was still playing the part of the corporate wife and mother. She was such a workaholic during the time she worked for a computer company, she burned out. I would have gone crazy if I had stayed home full time, but there was no arguing with her happiness.

Emily's voice interrupted my reverie.

"Our dresses for the wedding arrived yesterday," Emily said. "Grandma Rae works miracles in fabric."

"My dress twirls," said Elizabeth.

The food arrived and silence reigned while we savored each bite.

Elizabeth fell asleep on the ride home. I strained under the weight of carrying my six year old into the house and laying her on the bed.

"I'm at the exciting part of the book I'm reading," Emily said. "I'm going to take out my contact lenses, get ready for bed, and read."

"Okay, sweetie, you're a chip off the old block."

I went into the kitchen and took the gallon jug of English Breakfast tea from the refrigerator and poured some over a glass of ice. It was called "sun tea" because of the way it's made: filling a large glass container with cold water, placing many tea bags at the top of the water, then setting it outside. The Arizona sunshine heats the water and brews the tea.

I settled down at the kitchen table to read reviews in *Booklist* and mark those I wanted for my library.

An hour later I heard Dan's car pull into the driveway, heralded by the dogs in the neighborhood. I met him and Paco at the door.

"How are the tuxedos?"

"Tailored to fit," Dan said. "We also rented some black patent leather shoes and went to Target to get black socks before I took Eric and Nick back to Diana's."

"Is it okay if I take a shower tonight, before going to bed?" Paco asked as he started toward the back room.

"Sure," I said. "I'll wake you up a little later tomorrow morning."

I'm ready to take off my clothes and watch the news," Dan said. "I'll join you in a minute."

I went into the kitchen and put the magazines into the crate which I carried back and forth to work.

I walked into my bedroom. Dan and I slept in the four-poster bed Rob and I bought when we were married seventeen years ago. Even though we're both tall, the full-size bed suited us. We usually slept spoon style, so there was plenty of room. Dan was lying on the top of the floral quilt.

*   *   *

The rehearsal dinner was the next night at my house. I kept it simple with Price Club lasagna, salad, and bakery cheesecake. There were so many people I didn't remember conversations with any of them.

The next morning Susan and I, both wearing jeans and sweatshirts, were seated in a booth at "The Good Egg" on Tenth Street and Camelback, waiting for Carol. The waitress set down a teapot of hot water with a bag of Twinings English Breakfast Tea in front of me, poured a cup of coffee for Susan, and left the pot.

"You look sick!" I cried after taking a good look at my friend.

"I feel crappy, too. My throat is sore, my eyes are itchy, and my nose is running."

"Sounds like an allergy. Your hotel is in an orange grove. Are you allergic to oranges in your middle age?"

"I don't know. Where can I see a doctor so the sneezing doesn't spoil the wedding?"

I told her about the clinic at St. Joseph's hospital.

"So, what's your story?" I asked.

"I checked out public schools for Vanessa. There are two in our area. I ruled one out when I visited. The other school is okay, but nothing great. David and I have decided to look into private schools."

"I know the public schools have problems, but you need to be part of the solution. You would make a terrific school board member."

"Not me, David maybe. The problems in California are not ones that can be solved by a school board. There just isn't enough money going into education. I don't like the elitism of a private school, but I don't want Vanessa to suffer."

"In any school, it all comes down to the individual teacher," I said. "A principal can help make the school better, but basically it's the teacher and the students for seven hours a day. I have to make a decision soon.'

'Hey, have you heard anything from Dr. Trejo about when our book is coming out?"

"I saw him at a library conference. He said it should be out in time for the American Library Association Conference at the end of June. I asked him to send both of us forty copies, charged to our royalties."

"*The Castle of Chuchurumbel* retold by Annie Weissman, illustrated by Susan Bailyn. That has a great ring to it" Susan said. "May it be the first of many professional collaborations."

We clinked water glasses in a toast.

I spotted Carol rushing into the restaurant and waved her over to our booth. I turned a mug right side up and poured her a cup of coffee. Susan got up and gave Carol a big hug.

"It's so good to see you," Carol said. "I just finished watching Patrick's soccer game. His team lost but he scored the only goal. He may look like his dad but he's got my athletic ability."

The waitress came over and we all ordered veggie eggs Benedict, with no mushrooms for me.

"How are you doing?" Susan asked Carol.

"I've got an announcement. You are looking at the executive director of Safe House, an agency that runs a shelter for battered women."

"All right! A toast for your new job!" Susan said. We lifted our mugs.

Carol smiled and said, "Yes! It's a smaller agency and I shouldn't have to work seventy hours a week. And how are you feeling, Miss Annie, on the day of your wedding?"

"I'm shocked at how calm I am. I was a nervous wreck when I married Rob. This time it's easier, even though we planned and paid for it ourselves."

"I didn't get a chance to talk to Dan last night at the rehearsal dinner," Susan said. "I can't believe you're marrying someone on whom I haven't passed judgment."

"I already gave my stamp of approval," Carol said.

"Dan's kids seemed a little wild last night," Susan said.

"They were just excited to see their grandparents, aunts and uncles," I said. "They're great kids. The Brady Bunch is alive and lives at my house."

"Those boys are lucky to be getting you for a step mom. I'm glad you're happy."

"I have some words of wisdom about marriage for you," Carol said, pausing for effect. "I think I'm entitled since it took me three times before I got it right. The old adage 'never go to sleep angry' is true. Make sure you don't let the walls build up between you and Dan. Every time a few bricks get in place, take the time to talk about it. Don't sweep the problems under the rug."

"Carol, I'm impressed!" Susan said.

"I know how happy, safe, and content I am with Terry and I wish the same for you, Annie." Carol leaned over and squeezed my shoulder.

"Okay, wedding breakfast stuff done, now, have you heard any good gossip?"

The rest of the coffee klatch revolved around current news and digging up memories of years ago.

*   *   *

I stood at the entrance to the Mountain Shadows Country Club garden, half listening to the nondescript bubbly piano music, dressed in my cream silk and lace wedding gown. A last look in the mirror of the ladies room had confirmed the unbelievable. I looked beautiful. My hairdresser and the makeup artist had used their skills to compliment my best features. Although I was forty pounds heavier than at my first wedding, seventeen years before, the new wedding gown adeptly camouflaged the extra weight.

The guests were seated in rows of folding chairs on the garden's green velvet grass. The brick walkway led to the other side of the garden where Dan, his brothers Bob and Steve, Nick, and Eric were dressed in matching gray tuxedos. Eric had an impish grin on his face, perhaps from embarrassment at having to hold a frilly pillow with the wedding rings. Paco was also in a tuxedo, ushering people to seats.

A profusion of fuchsia and white petunias toppled over the rounded edge of the brick flowerbed in the middle of the garden. The shrubs and trees behind Dan were decked with tiny white Christmas lights. Large globes were strung over the heads of the guests to provide light on the March evening.

Elizabeth walked down the aisle, carefully measuring her steps, trying not to trip over her long, billowing, blue dress. Her hair was done in a sophisticated style, with huge curls cascading from the back of her head. The hairdo clashed with her typical six-year old smile. Half of her front teeth were missing and a retainer was working on the new crooked ones.

Emily looked beautiful. The peach dress, with a satin sash and big bow on the dropped waist, and her bobbed hairstyle were reminiscent of the high society salon look of the roaring twenties. I could no longer deny that my older daughter was becoming a young woman. She would be thirteen in June.

Susan, wearing a lavender lace dress, walked with poise down the aisle. Evvy, my sister and matron of honor, made her way toward the rest of the wedding party. Her closely tailored pink suit fit her executive image.

I wondered why I wasn't nervous. I was marrying a man I'd known for less than seven months. I was taking on the responsibility of two more children. Many of my friends didn't like Dan. But he'd taught me to do what I wanted and not worry about what others think. I respected him. I liked him. I trusted him. I loved him. I was ready.

The pianist banged out the Wedding March. Everyone turned to watch me. "Look at that smile!" I heard Carol say. "She looks like a guru who's just figured out the meaning of life."

The judge began to read the wedding service I had written. She stopped at one point and Emily took her silver flute from the glass table behind her, put it to her lips, and started to play. The first part sounded stilted and mechanical.

She plays much better than that, I thought, she's probably scared, poor thing. Then the music started to flow, with Emily's emotions heard through the lilting melody.

The judge continued the ceremony and I listened to the poetry. I wanted Dan and I to read the poems, but Dan drew the line there. He was not going to spout poetry in front of his golf buddies. I knew the Shakespearean sonnet by heart:

> "Let me not to the marriage of true minds
> Admit impediments. Love is not love
> Which alters when it alteration finds,
> Or bends with the remover to remove.
> Oh no! It is an ever-fixed mark
> That looks on tempests and is never shaken.
> It is the star to every wandering bark,
> Whose worth's unknown, although his height be taken.
> Love's not Time's fool though rosy lips and cheeks
> Within his bending sickle's compass come.
> Love alters not with his brief hours and weeks,
> But bears it out even to the edge of doom.
> If this be error and upon me proved,
> I never writ, nor no man loved."

We repeated our vows and the deed was done.

After the photographer was done with the bridal party, Dan and I danced to "Strangers in the Night." I snuggled close to him and happiness seeped from my body's cells. The guests joined us on the dance floor and the celebration started.

Later Dan got into an impromptu card game in the men's locker room for a short while, just to be polite, he told me.

By eleven-thirty the guests were leaving. Carol and Terry were trying to take Elizabeth, Emily, and Paco back to their house for the night, but Elizabeth was resisting. I kissed Elizabeth again and walked her to Carol's car.

"I want to stay with you, Mommy," Elizabeth said.

"You can't. It's my wedding night and I'm staying here with Dan. We'll come over tomorrow morning and pick you up."

"No! I want to be with you!" Elizabeth wailed and started to cry.

I had to push Elizabeth into the car. Emily held her while they locked the doors.

"She's just tired, Mom, she'll be okay," Emily said through the window.

As Terry drove his car out of the parking lot, I could still hear Elizabeth yelling, "Mommy! Mommy!" and mother's guilt stuck in my throat and made it hard to swallow.

Dan put his arm around me and kissed me on the forehead. "She'll be fine," he said.

We went back inside, said the last goodbyes, and went up to our room. Dan helped me unbutton my dress. He took off his tuxedo and hung it up, then folded back the covers and sheets on the king sized bed.

"God damn it!" he said, but he was laughing. I turned around to see him sweeping something onto the floor.

"What's wrong?"

"Somebody put frosted flakes in the bed! Better watch out when you use the toilet. There's no telling what they've done in the bathroom. My brother must have taught the kids his tricks."

I inspected the toilet. Someone had put Saran wrap across it, underneath the seat.

"You're right! They struck in here too. Anything else they might have done?"

"No, that's probably it."

I changed into a see-though, white, short nightgown I had found at Frederick's of Hollywood. I walked out of the bathroom and modeled it for Dan, who was already in bed.

"What's that supposed to be?" he asked.

"This little number is supposed to drive you wild."

"You don't need *that* to look sexy. You look just fine with nothin' on."

I shrugged my shoulders, took off the nightie, and climbed into bed, accepted exactly as I was.

*   *   *

I called my mother the next week to describe all the details of the ceremony and the reception.

"It was perfect, Mom. The girls loved the dresses you made for them. Emily looked so grown up and sophisticated in hers and Elizabeth's dress fit perfectly, including the hem. She and Eric were just adorable together going down the aisle. The judge did a nice job but I'm still hurt that the rabbi wouldn't marry us because Dan isn't Jewish. I've been a member of the temple for five years and it is a Reformed congregation. I wish that you and Pops could have been there."

"I wish I could have been there too, but I couldn't take a chance that your Dad would get worse while I was in Arizona."

"I know, Mom."

"Your father appreciated the letters you've written him. He had forgotten about that day you two went fishing until you jogged his memory."

"May I talk to Daddy?"

"Sure, let me give him the phone."

"Hiya Baby."

"Hi Pops. How are you?"

"I'm feeling weak but glad to be home from the hospital for a while."

"I'm doing my principal internship this week in Chandler in a brand new elementary school. Today the principal let me do some observations and feedback sessions with teachers. I think I might really like administration."

"You'll make a great principal and an even better superintendent."

"Pops, don't get too far ahead. I haven't even started applying for assistant principal jobs yet."

"I know you'll do it. Students and teachers need you."

"Thanks for the vote of confidence."

"I'm tired, I need to lie down."

"Hope you feel better, Daddy."

I put the receiver on its cradle. I knew he was slipping away and I felt helpless.

*   *   *

At the wedding. From left to right: Emily, Eric, Dan, Nick, Elizabeth, with Annie in front

CHAPTER 8

If I can stop one heart from breaking,
I shall not live in vain;
If I can ease one life the aching,
Or cool one pain,
Or help one fainting robin
Unto his nest again,
I shall not live in vain.

-Emily Dickinson

Emily's bat mitzvah was at ten in the morning on the last Saturday of May. I planned a buffet luncheon after the service. My friends were cooking platters of delicacies, knowing my ineptitude in the kitchen. The champagne for mimosas was chilling in the refrigerator, along with the orange juice. Sets of bar glasses, recent wedding presents, were sparkling clean and lined up on the bar.

The folding chairs and card tables had been delivered by the rental company the day before. I had sewn the pink and blue tablecloths, twelve in all. Pink and blue flowered plants, in pots covered by gold foil, served as the table centerpieces.

After the luncheon, we would have six hours to wash the tablecloths, rearrange the furniture, and create a nightclub atmosphere for the party for Emily's friends. I was grateful that Susan had flown in for the occasion, for the moral and artistic support.

Emily was very concerned about her appearance for the big day.

My mother had bought material for a bat mitzvah dress, but she hadn't had time to sew it because Daddy had been in the hospital so much. Instead she had sent me the money to buy a dress. Emily had picked out a blue, flowered, polished cotton, princess style dress from the Laura Ashley store.

I had taken Emily to the cosmetics counter at a department store so the consultant could show her how to apply an appropriate amount of makeup. And Emily had convinced the orthodontist not to put on the braces until the first week of summer vacation.

"Let's go!" I shouted.

Susan emerged from the back bedroom and said, "I'm ready!"

Elizabeth came running out in her dress and sneakers.

"Elizabeth, go back in your room, put on white tights and the white patent leather shoes you wore to the wedding."

"I don't want to wear tights. It's too hot!"

I gave her one of my "you better follow my directions now" looks.

"Okay, but you have to buckle the shoes," she said as she stomped away.

"How do I look, Mom?" Emily asked.

I studied her. My Emily was poised and grown up. And beautiful. The dress brought out the blue in her eyes, her auburn hair shone, and the makeup was not noticeable.

"You are going to wow everyone with how great you look and how well you conduct the service."

Elizabeth came in, clumping her feet in the white Mary Jane shoes. I bent down, buckled the shoes and said, "Let's move it on out!"

The temple sanctuary was filled almost three quarters full with friends of Emily and mine and other congregants. I was disappointed that none of Emily's extended family would be there to witness one of the most important events in her life. Even if Daddy hadn't been so sick, he wouldn't have attended. He was not enamored of religious rituals. I didn't know why Rob's parents hadn't come. All of the aunts and uncles lived out of town and had declined their invitations. At least Susan and Carol were there to stand in for the family.

I joined Dan and his boys in the front row.

The rabbi, the cantor, and Emily conducted the service. Emily did an outstanding job. Susan and I were called to the Torah and recited the *alliyah* Emily had taught us. At the end of the service, Emily thanked everyone and I gave a short speech about her. I said Emily was true to her inner self, and I sang "This Little Light of Mine, I'm Going to Let It Shine," exhorting her to use her talents and be proud of them.

At the house, afterward, Emily's father, his girlfriend, and her children sat at a table alone. I could understand how uncomfortable he felt, surrounded by my friends who sent dagger looks his way. I wasn't angry at Rob, anymore, just disappointed our love couldn't overcome obstacles.

After the guests left, Dan went to pick up the helium canister and the balloons. I took out the sign I had worked on during the weekends Emily spent with Rob. I plugged it in the socket. The three foot by five foot white foam board lit up with white Christmas tree lights and pink and blue paint that spelled out "Emily".

"Do you like it?"

"It's great, Mom! Thanks!" Emily said as she hugged me.

"Okay, let's get cracking. Nick and Eric, take the tablecloths off the tables and shake them out on the porch, then put them in the washing machine. Susan, how do you want to rearrange the furniture?"

Friends stopped by to help as we worked for hours. We moved the dining room furniture to form a dance floor and the disc jockey's space. We inflated pink, blue, and white balloons, fooling around with the helium to sound like munchkins. We made centerpieces with the balloons held by pink and blue curled ribbons that were anchored in small blue bags illustrated with brown teddy bears and pink ribbons. Elizabeth and Eric sprinkled tiny blue and pink metallic teddy bears on each table. Pots of flowers were arranged on the pie cooler. The pink and blue teddy bear cake, ordered from a parent at my school, was placed in a position of honor at the food table, along with the silver serving dish of bonbons, all white except the pink ones making a capital "E."

Nick, Paco, and Patrick filled small acrylic jars with candy. Emily placed the jars, on which she and I had painted the guests names written in pink or blue, on the tables as place cards and gifts.

Dan brought home the six foot submarine sandwich and set

up ice chests with different kinds of pop. When it was almost time for the party to begin, Dan took the three younger children out for dinner and then to the roller skating rink. The boys would go home and Elizabeth and Dan would stay at Carol's until the party was over.

After they left, Emily came into the living room, which was now disguised as a nightclub, "Club Em." We had stolen many of the ideas from my niece's elaborate sweet sixteen party the year before. She looked at the floor.

"We need to talk, Mom. I would rather that you go visit Carol now. Susan can chaperone."

I felt like she had slapped me.

"What are you talking about, Emily?"

"I just think we'd have a better time at the party if you weren't here."

I looked at Susan, who lifted her eyebrows.

"If you insist, I will leave," I said, "but I'm going next door to Karlene's."

Anger and sadness fought for control of my emotions. How dare Emily banish me from the party? Hadn't I worked my butt off to make it look terrific? Hadn't I saved my hard earned money to pay for this extravaganza?

I knew that this was the first of many clashes as Emily strove for independence. But this hurt to my toes!

I ran next door where Karlene allowed me to rant and rave.

After an hour and a half, Susan came over to report that all was going well and Emily would allow me to come over for a few minutes to see the party in high gear.

The house was almost dark. The disc jockey's strobe light distorted my vision. There was popcorn all over my beautiful parquet floors. The kids were laughing and dancing wildly. I understood why Emily had wanted me to leave. I would not have allowed the scene before me to happen but the situation was not out of control. The kids were just having a good time. I went over to Emily, hugged her, and headed out the back door to Karlene's house.

Emily was serious about her bat mitvah

At the temple Back row (left to right): Paco, Annie, Dan Middle row:
Nick and Emily Front row: Elizabeth and Eric

Friends helped with the setup for the kids' party in the evening: (left to right) Susan G., Marcy, Carol, Annie, Susan B.

*   *   *

It was June. Three more days of school and the last one was a half day. I was working on the book inventory. The annual report was all done except for the last few statistics. Hallelujah! I was looking for some missing books when Mrs. Easton, Paco's homeroom teacher, stuck her head into my room and motioned me to the door.

"Paco isn't here yet. He's missed the two other graduation practices. If he doesn't show up today, he won't be allowed to participate in the ceremony tomorrow. Do you know where he is?"

"I haven't seen him this week. Did you call his mother?" I asked.

"The phone's been disconnected."

"I'll see if I can track him down. When's the practice?"

"It's at one o'clock, when they finish cleaning the cafeteria floor after lunch."

I headed to the office.

"Judy, I'm leaving campus on school business. Do I need to talk to the principal?"

"It's okay, she knows why you're leaving."

I drove to Paco's apartment. As I walked up to the door, I kicked beer cans out of the way. I knocked. No one answered. I knocked harder. No one answered. I banged on the door and yelled, "It's Ms. Weissman. I need to talk to you!"

I waited another minute. I was about to leave when I heard noises behind the door.

"I'm coming! Hold on, hold on," said a hoarse voice I recognized as Paco's mother's. The door opened a few inches.

"Paco hasn't been in school this week. Is he here?"

"No, that good for nothing left on Friday and hasn't been back."

"Do you have any idea where he is? If he isn't at graduation practice today, he won't be in the ceremony tomorrow."

"I knew that idiot wouldn't graduate."

"He'll still be promoted, but he won't get to be in the ceremony. Do you know where he might be?"

"He may be at his uncle's house. It's on Seventeenth Place, just north of Buckeye. It's a blue trailer."

"Thanks, I'll try that. If I find him, is it okay if he spends the night at my house tonight?"

"I don't care."

"Graduation is at nine o'clock tomorrow morning. I hope you can come."

I went back to my car and headed to Buckeye Road. I was glad it was nine-thirty in the morning because the area was dangerous after dark. I slowed down as I passed Fifteenth Avenue and found Seventeenth Place. It was a dirt road. I parked in front of the blue trailer.

There were no signs of life. I looked at the other buildings near by. They were boarded up but cars outside indicated they were occupied, probably crack houses. It was 100 degrees outside, but my sweat was more from fear than the heat.

I took a deep breath and walked up to the door and knocked hard.

"Who's there?" called out a gruff voice.

"It's Ms. Weissman, the librarian at Paco's school. I need to talk to Paco. It's an emergency."

The door opened and a man in his mid twenties stood there, squinting at the daylight. He had on soiled cutoffs. Missing teeth added nothing to his drugged, vacant look.

"I'm Ms. Weissman, the librarian at Paco's school. I need to speak with him; it's an emergency," I repeated.

The man peered at me with bloodshot eyes. "You're his teacher?" He shook his head from side to side, then closed the door.

I wasn't sure if I should knock again. I hesitated.

The door opened again and Paco appeared in his boxers. His hair was going in all directions and his pupils were dilated.

"Get your clothes on, Paco. You need to come with me right now."

Paco did not argue. He disappeared for a few minutes, then came out of the house dressed in a filthy white t shirt and baggy black shorts.

"Hey man, where're we goin'?"

"We're going to get you some clean clothes and a shower before you go back to school for graduation practice. I will not allow you to cheat yourself out of the graduation and the honors you deserve."

Paco sat quietly as we drove to Park Central Mall. Paco tried on shorts, dress shirts, and dress pants until we found one of each that fit and he liked. I bought him six pairs of boxers, tube socks, and white tee shirts, knowing that they might not survive a week at his house before someone appropriated them. I used my charge card since I had no money. It was three days before I received my summer checks. We stopped at the drug store to pick up some lice shampoo. I had spied a live one when he came out of the dressing room in Penney's.

When we went back to my house, Paco took a shower and used the lice shampoo. He wore a towel around his shoulders as I used the small comb, included with the shampoo, to comb the dead bugs out of his hair. I shuddered at the black dots on the pink towel. I used my fingernails to pick out the few eggs I saw. I went over many sermons and heart to heart talks in my head, but they remained unspoken.

"I made some sandwiches while you were in the shower. Finish getting dressed and you can eat the sandwiches and a Coke in the car on the way back to school."

As I parked the car at the school lot, Paco turned to me and softly said, "Thanks."

That was enough for me.

"I asked your mother if you could spend the night with us. Is that okay with you?"

"Sure," he said.

"Good. Come to the library after school."

* * *

There was a full house for the graduation ceremony. I was there to see Paco graduate. His mother, her boyfriend, his father and stepmother and all of his brothers and sisters were there to share in Paco's honor. I knew that he was going to get a $100 scholarship to North High to be used to rent his books for the International Baccalaureate program.

Tears crowded my eyes when it was Paco's turn to get his diploma. He had made it, the second person in his family to graduate from eighth grade. The memory of the blue trailer on Seventeenth Place flashed into my head. High school graduation was going to be harder to achieve. Paco was bright enough to be a valedictorian, but might not be able to resist the outside temptations. I vowed to have him stay with us for most of the summer to keep him out of trouble. It would be a full house with Nick and Eric all summer, too.

* * *

Paco at his eighth grade graduation

CHAPTER 9

Presentiment is that long shadow on the lawn

-Emily Dickinson

Two days later my mother called to ask if we were planning to visit soon.

"No. What's wrong?"

"I think it would be a good idea for you to come to New York to see Dad. Bring Elizabeth and Emily."

"Mom, tell me what's going on."

"Annie, your father's been in the hospital for five days with no sign of getting better. The doctor suggested that you bring the children while his head is still clear."

"Oh my God! I'll make reservations right away. Where are you staying?"

"Walter is letting me stay at his studio apartment while he's in Europe. It's two blocks from the hospital. There isn't enough room for you and the girls."

We took the red eye flight to New York. The trip was exhausting. Elizabeth wanted my attention every minute. Emily read a book and pretended she didn't know us. By the time we got off the plane I could not tell one more story or play one more game of "Go Fish".

We arrived in the dark and dingy lobby of our hotel. The furniture consisted of one old brown couch and a cracked, ripped, green leather chair. The desk looked like it was from an old movie set. I took a deep breath and approached the desk clerk.

"We have reservations. The name is Weissman."

The clerk studied a ledger until he found it.

"We weren't expecting you until tomorrow," he said.

"I just made the reservations yesterday. We'll be staying for two nights."

"Well, we do have a room available. Just fill out this card. I need a credit card imprint."

I filled out the card while Emily amused Elizabeth. An overstuffed bellman approached.

"We don't have much luggage. We'll be able to manage our bags."

The bellman scowled and turned away with a pivot of his foot.

The room was barely adequate. The carpet was threadbare. A trip into the bathroom showed dirt in the corners and hair in the drains.

"Mom! Look!" shouted Elizabeth. "Our window shows a brick wall!"

"That's not unusual in New York City," I said. "Let's walk over to the hospital and see Grandpa Ben. We won't be able to stay long because he's sick. We'll go to Central Park. It's near the hospital. Let me show you the picture I took of Grandpa Ben in December. He doesn't have any hair and he looks older."

I took the picture out of the side compartment of my pocketbook and passed it to Emily, but Elizabeth grabbed it. She glanced at it before handing it over to her sister.

"It's hard to believe how different he looks," Emily said.

"I know," I said softly. "He'll be so happy to see the three of us. That's why we came, to talk to him, and cheer him up."

The walk to Mt. Sinai was short but hot. We welcomed the coolness inside the hospital. I didn't ask the age requirement for visitors, but quickly walked towards an open elevator. As the doors opened on the fourth floor, the antiseptic and dying smells hit me in the face.

We found my father's room without asking for directions or drawing attention to ourselves. I took a deep breath for courage and pushed on the door.

"Grandpa!" Elizabeth shouted. She ran to the hospital bed and hopped up to give the shriveled man a hug and kiss.

"Hi Grandpa," Emily said as she moved slowly towards the bed and took his hand in hers.

I was speechless at the sight of my father. His head and shoulders were sticking out of the many blankets on the bed. He seemed to have shrunk in all directions. Get over it! I scolded myself. We're here to make him feel good.

"Hi Daddy," I said as I leaned over and kissed his saggy, paper-thin cheek.

"I'm so glad you're here, Annie girl," he said.

"Where's Mom?"

"She went back to the apartment to take a shower. She stayed with me last night."

"Can I eat your Jello, Grandpa?"

I noticed the untouched food tray next to the bed.

"Can you or may you?" my father asked Elizabeth. "You are capable of eating it but I think you're asking my permission. You need to ask 'May I eat your Jello?'"

"May I eat your Jello?" asked a chastened Elizabeth.

"Yes, you may."

I laughed and said, "I'm glad to see you're still up to correcting everyone's grammar."

"It's a losing battle these days, even the newscasters use split infinitives."

"Why do you have a needle in your arm, Grandpa?" asked Elizabeth.

"The needle hooks up to these bags of medicine. The medicine goes straight into my body. So what are you doing with yourself this summer, Emily?" my father whispered.

"I'm going to an Actor's Workshop for three weeks this summer. We learn acting, singing, and dancing. We put on a show at the end of the three weeks that's listed in the entertainment section of the *Arizona Republic*. Then I'm going to Camp Pacific for five days with the band from school. We'll work on the pieces we're going to play at the Arizona State Fair in the fall. The last day we spend at Disneyland from the time it opens until it closes."

"I'm sorry that you won't be able to spend the usual two weeks with us. I never know when I'll go into the hospital. Are you going to visit your other grandparents?"

"Yes, Daddy is taking us to Ohio for two weeks in August."

"I'm doing things too, Grandpa Ben. Mommy signed me, Nick, and Eric up to take a class at the Indian ruins for a week," Elizabeth said. "We're also on the swim team at the pool near our house. Eric and I play t-ball on the same team. Nick and Eric are living with us, and sometimes Paco, too. And we're going to go fishing for a week with Carol's family."

"It sounds like a busy summer for you. I'm tired and need to sleep."

"Do you want us to stay until Mom gets back?" I asked.

"No, I'll be fine,"

As we left the room, I looked back at my father. He was already asleep.

As soon as we were out of the hospital, I breathed in deeply. It might be polluted, but New York smelled like life, filled with garlic, sweat, and exhaust fumes. We walked to the Central Park Zoo. I thought back to almost thirty years ago, when I showed off the zoo to Susan as if I were the proprietor. It was our first trip into the city alone.

"These animals look sad," Emily said. "They don't have much room in the cages."

"I like this zoo!" Elizabeth said. "I can get closer to the animals. In the Phoenix Zoo the animals hide at the back of their areas."

The zoo looked dirtier and more decrepit than I remembered.

"How about hot dogs?"

Both girls nodded yes.

We found a vendor outside the zoo and ate on a park bench.

"Let's go back to the hospital and see Grandpa Ben. Maybe Grandma Rae will be there too."

We walked quickly to keep up with the flow of human traffic on the sidewalk. No one questioned me about bringing children into the hospital. My mother was sitting in a chair, reading, when we entered the hospital room.

I gave her a long hug.

"And who do you have with you?"

"It's us, Nana Rae!" Elizabeth said, as she flung herself into her grandmother's arms.

Emily walked over and gave her grandmother a hug and kiss.

"He's sleeping now. Why don't we get an ice cream."

"That's a great idea, Mom." I was eager to leave the sickening smells of the hospital.

The four of us sat in a small stationery store, eating ice cream. My mother indulged the girls with double scoops. The store reminded me of one in Teaneck where Susan and I went every day after school for a snack. There weren't any stores in Phoenix that sold only candy, ice cream, greeting cards, and school supplies.

"So how does he look to you?" my mother asked.

"He seems in good spirits but very tired and small," I said.

"Yes, he's down to 115 pounds. He was going through a depression. Your visit has brought him up quite a bit."

"But we only stayed a few minutes," Emily said.

"He felt your love, that's what's important. Tomorrow you can visit him again. Come over after breakfast, go to the planetarium, then come back to visit him.

I let Elizabeth and Emily stay up late, watching old movies on television. Although we were physically exhausted, none of us could fall asleep. At midnight I turned off the television and tucked the girls into bed. I stayed awake a long time, digging for memories to use in conversation with my father the next day.

I remembered dinner time, playing "College Bowl," discussing politics, and the civil rights projects my parents were active in. My father would sit at the head of the table. After we finished eating, we would pass our plates his way and he would eat the leftovers. We called him the "human garbage disposal." He would gather up the crumbs after the dishes were removed. On the few times he got angry, he would say, "For crying out loud!" and wad up his paper napkin and throw it on the crumbs, which would fly in all directions with a "poof".

My family was the model of what a family was supposed to be: loving, fun, supportive. Susan was close to my parents, and spent much of her childhood and adolescence at my house. My dad was strong in character and body, an intellectual giant, a comedian, a lecturer.

The girls and I visited him for three days, then flew home. He didn't die; he hung on to life. Mom refused to let him go.

*   *   *

CHAPTER 10

They might not need me—yet they might—
I'll let my Heart be just in sight—
A smile so small as mine might be
Precisely their necessity—

-Emily Dickinson

The third Saturday in July Carol and I drove my extra long van, filled with kids and supplies, to Show Low, a town in Arizona's White Mountains. I got the van to replace my Toyota, which I had totaled at the end of May, driving Emily and Elizabeth to school. Luckily no one was hurt.

Patrick, Carol's son, and Paco spent most of the ride playing poker. Emily attempted to read and referee while Nick, Eric, and Elizabeth played games.

"This is it!" I said as we drove into the driveway of a small house on the outskirts of town.

Everyone got out to inspect the cabin that would be our home for the next week. It was clean and decorated in the country cute style. The living room had a television, two couches and a rocking chair. There were two bedrooms. One was a dormitory with three sets of bunk beds, each with a comforter of a different material. The other room was small, just big enough for one full-size bed. The kitchen contained the basics. The bathroom had a small stall shower and I prayed the plumbing would work even when taxed to the limit with ten people.

The children started to fight over beds.

"Work it out yourselves or I'll assign beds," I said in my teacher voice.

"Terry and I will sleep on the fold-out couch in the living room," Carol offered. "You newlyweds can have the private bedroom."

"That's okay, we'll sleep on the couch," I said.

Carol lowered her voice and said, "We need to sleep in the living room to make sure Patrick doesn't sneak out during the night."

"Oh Lord, Carol, you went through enough with Zobi's antics."

"I'm not positive it's going on," Carol whispered, "but I'll sleep better if I'm between him and the door."

I opened my mouth, then shut it. Now was not the time to remind Carol there was a back door.

With so many pairs of hands, it didn't take long to unload the van.

"When's my dad going to be here?" Nick asked.

"He'll be here tonight, after you go to sleep. He's driving up with Terry, after he gets off work. You'll see him in the morning."

The children went to investigate the woods behind the cabin while Carol and I put dinner together.

"I made the chili mild and baked plain cornbread. I know your crew isn't into spicy or unusual food," Carol said as she plopped the chili into a pot on the stove.

It was eight o'clock by the time dinner was cleaned up. I supervised and helped as the children put sheets on the dormitory beds. Elizabeth, Nick, and Eric got into their pajamas. I told them the story of "The Crab and the Jaguar". Emily listened with one ear while she read.

"Once upon a time there was a crab who lived by the sea. When he got bored, he would play a game with his eyes.

"Eyes," he would say, "little eyes of mine, fly away to the big blue sea."

His eyes would leap out of their sockets and run away to the deep blue sea.

Then he would call out, "Eyes, little eyes of mine, comeback here from the deep blue sea!"

And his eyes would fly back into their sockets.

One day when he was playing this game, along came a jaguar.

"Oooh, that's a wonderful game!" said Mr. Jaguar. "Could you do it to my eyes?"

"Well, yes I could," said Mr. Crab, "but I won't. The terrible Animale Podole, the father of the Trehira fish, lives in the deep blue sea. If I send your eyes out there, he might eat them up."

"But he didn't eat your eyes," said Mr. Jaguar.

"I'm willing to risk my own eyes," said Mr. Crab, "but not someone else's."

Please!" begged Mr. Jaguar.

"No!" said Mr. Crab.

"Please!"

"No!"

"Please, please, please, please, please, please!"

"All right!" said Mr. Crab. "Eyes, eyes of Mr. Jaguar, run away to the deep blue sea, quick, quick, quick, quick, quick!"

The jaguar's eyes leaped out of their sockets and ran away to the deep blue sea. In a little while the crab called the eyes back.

"Eyes, eyes of Mr. Jaguar, come back here from the deep blue sea, quick, quick, quick, quick, quick!"

The eyes went back into the jaguar's face.

"Ooh, that was fun!" said Mr. Jaguar. "Do it again! Do it again!"

"I told you I can't," said Mr. Crab. "The terrible Animale Padole, the father of the trehira fish, lives in the deep blue sea. If I send your eyes out there, he may swim by and eat up your eyes."

"But he didn't do it, did he?" said Mr. Jaguar.

"Maybe not this time, but possibly the next time," said Mr. Crab.

"I'm willing to take the risk," said Mr. Jaguar. "Do it again! Do it again!"

"No!" said Mr. Crab.

"Please?" said Mr. Jaguar.

"No!"

"Please!"

"No!"

"Please, please, please, please, please, please!"

"All right!" said Mr. Crab. "Eyes, eyes of Mr. Jaguar, run away to the deep blue sea, quick, quick, quick, quick, quick!"

The jaguar's eyes leaped out of their sockets and ran away to the deep blue sea. Right to where the Animale Padole, the father of the trehira fish was swimming. He ate the jaguar's eyes.

Mr. Crab called, "Eyes, eyes of Mr. Jaguar, come back here from the deep blue sea, quick, quick, quick, quick, quick!"

Nothing happened.

Mr. Crab called again, "Eyes, eyes of Mr. Jaguar, come back here from the deep blue sea, quick, quick, quick, quick, quick!"

Nothing happened. The crab called many times but the jaguar's eyes did not come back.

Mr. Crab buried himself in the sand.

Mr. Jaguar finally realized that his eyes had been eaten by the Animale Padole. He wandered along the beach until he bumped into Mr. King-Vulture.

Mr. King-Vulture said, "Say, watch where you're going!"

"I can't!" said Mr. Jaguar. "Mr. Crab sent my eyes out to the sea and the terrible Animale Padole, the father of the trahira fish, ate them up. Say, you come across a lot of eyes on animal carcasses. Could you get me another pair of eyes?"

"Why should I?" asked Mr. King-Vulture.

"If you find me new eyes, whenever I kill something for my dinner, I'll leave some for you."

So the vulture flew off and found another pair of eyes for the jaguar. He brought them back. Mr. Jaguar popped them in place.

"These new eyes are even better than the old pair!" said Mr. Jaguar.

And that's why whenever a jaguar kills something for food, it always leaves some for the vultures.

Paco and Patrick played cards for a short time, but all the children fell asleep early.

I opened a bottle of Inglenook Chablis, poured two glasses, and joined Carol in the backyard.

We sat on lawn chairs, under the thick forest of pine trees that towered above, blocking out most of the stars. The pine needles and tall trunks looked dark gray in the pale moonlight. The crickets serenaded. And it was cool, blissfully cool. Such a welcome change from the suffocating Phoenix summer heat.

"It's so peaceful, it reminds me of my mountain in Colorado," Carol said. "Thanks for letting us tag along on your vacation, we really need one, but money is very tight. I keep making lovely budgets, but we don't stick to them. Terry and I earn a lot of money and enjoy spending even more. How are you doing with four children?"

"It's working out fine. I chauffeured them to summer programs so they didn't have time to get bored. Paco has been with us some of the summer, too. He'll stay with his mother starting next week when the other kids go to see grandparents.

Emily and Elizabeth leave for Ohio while Nick and Eric go to Missouri. We're meeting with Diana, Dan's ex-wife, next week. The boys say they want to live with us, not go back with her after the summer."

"You're kidding!"

"No, I hope they can stay."

"I've taken in stepchildren and been burned. Are you sure you want to take on that much responsibility?"

"I knew they would be living with us within a year of my marriage to Dan. Hell, the second time Nick saw me, he asked if he could live with Dan and me when we got married. Life is going so well, except for my dad being sick. Hey, did you hear that? I think the guys are here."

We ran around to the front of the cabin to see our husbands knock at the front door.

"It's open!" I yelled.

Terry jumped. "Yikes! You want to scare me to death?"

We laughed and helped unload the car. We sat under the tall pines, drinking wine for an hour, telling stories on each other.

"I'm going to bed," Dan announced.

"Guess I'll turn in too," I said.

"I don't want any loud noises from your room," Terry said. "You'll make me jealous."

"Don't worry," Carol said. "We'll make our own noises."

*　　*　　*

Dan got everyone up at five in the morning.

"You can't catch fish by sleeping away the day," he said.

After some grumbling over cereal, we went to Sheep's Meadow, at the base of Mount Baldy. Dan patiently baited hooks, over and over again, for Elizabeth and Nick. The other children could do their own. Paco caught the first trout. Then the fish started to bite and everyone caught at least one. By one o'clock, the fish were sleeping and so were Dan and Terry. Carol and I, gasping for breath, hiked up Mount Baldy with the kids.

That night Carol cooked the trout for dinner. Each child tried to identify and eat the fish he or she had caught. After dinner Paco and Patrick went outside. When Carol called to them an hour later, they were not around the cabin.

"Fuck!" said Carol. "I don't think I can handle another problem teenager."

Terry and Dan took the car and went looking for the two boys. They returned with Paco.

"Where were you?" I demanded. "I've been worried sick!"

"Patrick went to meet some girls so I went with him. The girls wanted us to go to a dance in town but I decided to come back."

"Please don't leave again without letting me know where you're going," I said.

"Okay," said Paco, looking at the floor.

"Do you know exactly where Patrick is?" Carol asked.

"The girls said the dance was at a church in Show Low. I'm tired. Is it okay if I go to bed?"

"Sure," I said.

"I'm not chasing all around town to find that boy," Terry said. "He'll come back and we'll talk tomorrow."

I didn't hear Patrick come in, but he was there for breakfast. His blond straight hair was sticking up at odd angles and his eyes were just slits. Carol was giving off looks that could freeze steam. After breakfast, Carol, Terry, and Patrick stayed behind at the cabin while the rest of us went fishing. At dinner, Patrick had a defiant look on his face. He didn't go outside after dinner.

Each day passed for us much like the one before: fishing in the morning, hiking and exploring in the afternoon.

"What a wonderful vacation!" Carol said the last evening, after the children had gone to bed. "You're right, Annie, your family is like the Brady Bunch. There are minor squabbles, but the kids get along very well."

"I finally feel like I've gotten to know Emily," Dan said. "We've had the time to talk. She's a very interesting person but it's like talking to an adult. Her vocabulary is better than mine."

"Another perfect chapter," I said.

"It just amazes me how well Paco fits in," Terry said. "You'd think he'd feel funny, but he made himself part of the group."

"He's a great kid. I'm nervous about his success in high school. They have an 'at risk' program at North High, but I wasn't impressed with the services. I'll have to keep a close eye on him. Maybe I'll ask him stay at our house during the week."

"That's fine with me," Dan said, "but I don't think he's going to be able to fit in with the nerds in that advanced program he's taking."

"Time will tell," I said. "It's late, let's hit the sack."

"Yeah, it's time," Terry said. "We've got a five hour drive ahead of us tomorrow."

A half hour later, after making love, Dan cuddled up to me. "I know I don't say this very often. I love you."

"I love you, Dan," I said as I kissed him on the cheek, savoring his whiskers on my lips.

*   *   *

The next week a large cardboard box arrived for me. The return address was "Hispanic Books Distributors".

"My book!" I shouted even though no one else was home.

I got a scissors to cut the strapping tape and quickly unwrapped the rectangle covered in newspaper.

I held up a copy of the picture book I had written and Susan had illustrated. I could feel the huge smile on my face as I opened *The Castle of Chuchurumbel/ el castillo de Chuchurumbel.*

I was a real author! I ran to the phone and called my dad, still in the hospital. He sounded weak but excited. I promised to send him a copy right away. Then I called my friends to have a celebratory luncheon.

*   *   *

Dan parked his car in the Coco's lot. He kept the engine on so the air conditioner would work. We were ten minutes early for our meeting with Diana, his ex-wife.

He turned to me and said, "Let's plan what we're going to say."

"I've been thinking about it, and thee are my suggestions. Don't say anything negative to her. Don't mention anything about her leaving the boys alone at night. First get her to agree that the boys should live with us, then try to get her to let go of child support. If you accomplish that, then ask her to pay some child support."

"That sounds good."

"Are you willing to pay her child support and have the boys live with us? It isn't fair, but if that is the only way to get them, would you agree?"

"I wouldn't like it, but I'd do it. I think you'd better do the talking. Every time I say something to her, we end up fighting."

"Oh Dan, I don't want the responsibility. What if I say the wrong thing and the boys go back to her?"

"I think your chances are better than mine to get her to approve. I know I'll say the wrong thing."

"Okay, but I wasn't prepared to do this. I don't guarantee anything."

As we approached the restaurant, Dan took my hand and squeezed it. We scanned the place and saw Diana sitting in a semicircular booth. Her head was down, almost to the coffee cup in front of her. We slid in the bench, with me next to Diana.

"Hi," I said.

"Hi," Diana answered, not looking up.

The next minute of silence seemed to last for days. I decided to go right to the point. Just as I opened my mouth, the waitress came to the table.

"I'll have an iced tea," I said.

"I'll have a Pepsi," Dan said.

"I'll have another cup of coffee," Diana said.

The waitress left and another silent minute dragged by. I took a deep breath and said, "We would like to arrange for Nick and Eric to live with us."

"I talked to the boys last night at my mother's house in Missouri," Diana said. "Nick said he wanted to live with you. Eric wasn't sure, but he wants to live with me. I don't think it's right for them to live separately."

"You're right," I said. "The boys should live together in either place. Just before they left for Missouri, Eric was the one who asked about living with us during the year. He said, 'Now that you and my Dad are married, when do we get to live with you all the time?'"

"He's never said that to me," Diana said.

I could hear the defensive tone in Diana's voice. Better back off, Annie.

The waitress returned with our drinks and the mundane interruption eased the tension, "Diana, what do you think of the boys living with us? You would still have joint custody. We'd change only the living arrangements."

"I have to think about what's best for them, not me. It's very hard for me to take care of them and work. And I know that boys need their father . . . . I need to know very soon because the lease on my apartment is up this month. I could save money if I rented a smaller place."

I knew she'd decided to allow Nick and Eric live with us if she was talking about moving to another apartment. I noticed her hands grasping the coffee cup, letting it go, then grasping it again. It had not been an easy decision.

"There's child care at the elementary school," I said. "It's called Cactus Club. Eric would stay there with Elizabeth until I picked them up at four o'clock. Nick would come home on the same bus with Emily. We'll all end up at home at about 4:15 every day."

"Are the schools good?"

"Yes, Emily and Elizabeth have had excellent teachers. We'll tell you about Open Houses and parent teacher conferences."

"I don't want to do it, but I think it will be best for Nick and Eric to have two parents," she said.

I studied Diana's face. There was some emotion reflected there, but it was hard to tell what: agony over the decision? self pity? embarrassment? guilt?

"You're making a hard decision, Diana. We'll pay for the lawyer to draw up the new papers and have them filed in court."

"What about the child support?"

I dreaded that question. It was only fair that she take financial responsibility, but this was not the time to suggest it. Diana had gotten the worldly goods from the marriage, after debts had been paid, because the children were going to stay with her. There was no use in going into all that.

"We'll file a motion to stop Dan from paying child support until the new order is worked out."

"Okay, but I'll want my lawyer to approve anything. When do you want to tell them?"

I hadn't thought about that. As I considered the question of who should tell the boys and when, the silence became tense.

Diana pushed the coffee cup and saucer away from her and said, "I'll tell them. I'm going back to Missouri on Saturday to see my parents and be with the boys. I'll say something to them then and give them time to get used to it. I've got to get back to work."

She hurried from the restaurant.

Dan smiled broadly and put his hand over mine.

"You were brilliant! How did you learn to talk like an attorney?"

"Remember, I was a negotiator for the teachers' association, and I helped Rob pass two Bar Exams. Dan, how could she do it?" Goose bumps came up on my arms.

"Do what?"

"I would never, ever, give up custody of my children. They are my life's breath. It's hard for me when they leave for the few weeks in the summer. Diana just gave up her children in a polite conversation in a coffee shop."

"She feels she's doing the best thing for them. She wants to work on her dreams, I guess."

"I guess . . . it's incomprehensible to me."

"I have an appointment I need to keep this afternoon, so I'll drop you off at home. But tonight I'm taking you out for a special thank you dinner. Thank you for wanting Nick and Eric to live with us. Thank you for loving them. Thank you for the way you take care of all that educational and cultural stuff. And thank you for talking today so Diana could agree without losing a battle with me."

I tried to kiss Dan as we left the restaurant but he ducked it. He hated public displays of attention. We would hug about it tonight, in bed. My heart swelled. I didn't have to hold back my love for the boys. I had four kids full time.

* * *

A week later, Dan woke me up at 3 a.m. He had terrible pain in his stomach. By 5 a.m. I convinced him to go to the hospital. Doctors kept insisting he was just full of gas and constipated and gave him several enemas, but nothing relieved the pain.

They finally did some other tests and found a pocket of infection in his colon. They wanted to operate.

"No way!" Dan said. "I want a second opinion!"

He was admitted to the hospital. The doctor started him on heavy duty intravenous antibiotics.

Dan called the "golf network." A golfing buddy knew a specialist, who came right over and examined Dan. He did not recommend surgery, but suggested Dan wait for four days to see if the antibiotics would clear up the problem.

Dan was a terrible patient. He complained about the pain from the IV and blood pressure checks. I brought the nurses boxes of candy to pacify them.

Finally the antibiotics worked and Dan left the hospital after six days. Of course he went right back to work and ate whatever he wanted.

CHAPTER 11

Goodbye to the Life I used to live—
And the World I used to know—

-Emily Dickinson

It was our last evening without children. Dan was stretched out on the long couch, drifting in and out of sleep. I was lying on the black recliner, watching "Sixty Minutes." Nick and Eric were in Missouri, visiting grandparents. Emily and Elizabeth were flying home with my ex-husband after visiting his parents in Ohio.

A message flashed across the bottom of the television screen, but I didn't see it soon enough to read it. Twenty minutes later another announcement flashed across the screen. "A Northwest Airlines plane crashed after take off from Detroit. The flight was due in Phoenix at 9:07 p.m."

I sat up straight in the chair, with my eyes locked on the television screen. Northwest flies from all over the world, the arrival time was just a coincidence, I told myself.

"It can't be Emily and Elizabeth's flight," I said, my heart beating wildly, "Someone would have called me. I'll call Rob's mom in Ohio, just to make sure."

Dan followed me into the bedroom.

As I strangled the receiver, someone answered and said Rob's parents couldn't come to the phone.

"I was just calling to put my mind at ease," I sputtered. "We're watching television and a news flash came across the bottom of the screen about a plane crash in Detroit."

"Yes, it was Rob's plane, that's why they can't come to the phone. They're too upset to talk to anyone." The voice sounded like a neighbor, annoyed that children were walking on her perfectly manicured lawn.

"NO! NO! NO! NO!" I screamed as I dropped the phone.

Dan picked up the phone.

"What's going on? . . . Holy shit! Didn't anyone think to call Annie?"

Dan hung up immediately and called Northwest Airlines. They refused to acknowledge anything but instructed him to go to the airport gate to get more information.

"I need help," he said. He called Carol and Terry to come over right away.

Dan came back and put his arms around me. I was rigid as a deer caught in headlights on the highway.

"I have to call my sister," I said as I dialed. "Evvy, I have very bad news. We think Emily, Elizabeth, and Rob were on the Northwest plane which crashed."

A long gray wail came from Evvy's end of the phone.

Dan spoke to her husband, who promised to get word to my parents in the hospital in New York City before they saw it on TV or read it in the newspaper. My sister agreed to tell the rest of the family.

Dan talked to Susan, Emily and Elizabeth's godmother, his face twisting like he was sucking on a lemon.

Dan turned on the television in the bedroom. The local news anchor reported, "There are very few details at this time. The only known survivor of the crash is a three or four year-old girl. Ambulances and fire trucks are at the scene."

The screen flashed on pictures of the debris at the crash sight. It looked like a bear had gotten in the garbage and strewn around what he didn't choose to devour.

"Dan, did they say only one survivor?" I asked, clutching at the hope that one of my daughters might have escaped death.

"Elizabeth has such a baby face she might be mistaken for a four year old even though she's seven." My whole body started to shake violently.

Dan left the room and returned with a shot glass.

"Drink this down in one gulp," he commanded.

As I drank the liquid fire, it flashed down my throat and out to my arms and legs. The shaking stopped but it was replaced with heaving sobs.

Dan put his arms around my back and hugged me. I could feel him swallow his own sob.

There was a knock at the door, Carol and Terry. They rushed into the bedroom.

"I'm going to the airport. Stay here with Carol," Dan ordered. "I'll call as soon as I know anything. Carol, please call Annie's friends. I'll phone my parents from the airport. Let's go, Terry, we'll take your car so you can drive."

Dan kissed my hair. Both men left.

Carol made the calls. I heard the words but didn't want to talk to anyone.

I got off the bed and went to the bathroom to splash some cold water on my face. Who was that woman in the mirror? My hair was disheveled, my eyes were bloodshot and swollen, the skin on my face slack. My mouth was set in a line, the muscles in my temple and jaw moved back and forth as I clenched and unclenched my teeth.

I went back to the bed and lay down with my face in the pillow, conjuring up the faces of my children. Emily. Reddish-brown hair that hung to her shoulders. Her creamy complexion was dotted with freckles that highlighted her pale, super intelligent, blue eyes. Elizabeth, a chubby-cheeked rascal with dancing, deep blue eyes, magnified by her tortoise shell glasses. A mouth of crooked teeth with the front three missing. Her brown hair curling in an unruly way about her face.

I lay very still on the bed. This can't be, I told myself over and over.

"I'm going to call the airlines myself," I blurted. "They probably wouldn't give Dan the information because he's not the nearest relative."

I picked up the phone and got the number from information. I dialed, punching the number buttons hard. The line was busy. I dialed it over and over again. Finally I got the number to ring, but heard only the hollowness of a prerecorded message.

"Carol, they're not answering the phones. The message says if you're meeting someone on flight 255 to go to the airport. Does that mean that the flight is coming in? Did the television give the wrong information? I have to get to the airport! They won't give Dan the information; they'll give it to me. I'm the mother!"

"I don't think that's a good idea, Annie. Dan will call us as soon as he knows anything."

"They won't tell him!" I screamed. I circled the bedroom like a lioness in a small steel cage, missing her cubs. "I'm going to the airport. Are you coming?"

"Annie, sit down, let's talk about this."

"I can't stay here anymore. I need to know what's happening. You can drive or I'll drive myself."

"I'd better drive. We'll have to take your car. Dan and Terry have mine."

I sat very still in the front seat, making deals with God.

The next thing I knew we were walking into the terminal at the airport. I saw Dan, ran and grabbed him for support.

There were three or four flashes. I looked up and saw a photographer taking pictures.

"Get out of here before I kill you!" Dan growled. He held me tighter in his arms, shielding my face.

"I just came from the meeting with the airline's representative," Dan whispered in my ear. "There was a crash. It's been confirmed that Emily, Elizabeth, and Rob were on the plane. There's only one survivor, a three year-old. Northwest gave us tickets to fly to Detroit tomorrow morning to help identify the remains."

"My babies . . . my babies . . . my babies . . . "

Dan kept his arms around me. I leaned on him heavily; my legs as unsteady as balloons that have lost their air. He led me out of the airport and took me home.

*　　*　　*

I didn't know if I'd slept or not. The line between the real and unreal was blurred. I tried not to think at all, but that was impossible.

Last night had to be a mistake, a terrible mistake. We would go to Detroit and find out that Rob had been late, as usual, and missed the flight. Thank God for his frailties! It wouldn't matter if Rob were two hours late picking up the girls next weekend. Then a voice inside me whispered, "It's true, they died." Sobs wracked my body.

I felt Dan move me into the spoon position. He seemed far away even though our bodies were touching. My stomach was a hard rock. It matched how my heart felt. I tried feeling, but the stabs of pain were unbearable. It was better to feel nothing at all.

"It's time to take a shower, Annie," Dan prodded. "We have to pack and get to the airport."

I stood in the shower and let the water run over my body, barely feeling the wetness. I made the water hotter and could see the steam, but the cascade felt lukewarm. I washed myself, scrubbing my arms hard with the washcloth, savoring the roughness. I still existed, but my babies didn't. I started heaving, not knowing or caring whether it was sobs or nausea.

I toweled dry and quickly put on my underwear, feeling exposed. I looked in my closet vacantly. What to bring to Detroit? All the bright colors of my clothing assaulted me.

I came to attention when Dan said, "Annie, you need to get dressed."

I was surprised to see myself still in my underwear. I quickly put on a pair of black jeans and a black shirt. I looked in my closet for a sweater and found a dark blue one.

"It's ninety degrees out, I don't think you need a sweater," Dan said.

"I feel cold."

My mind wandered again. The next time I was cognizant of my surroundings, we were walking towards a gate at the airport.

"This must be like getting on the horse that threw you," I muttered.

"What are you talking about?" Dan asked.

"It's very weird. An airplane to Detroit . . . identifying bodies . . . of my children . . . who died in an airplane crash."

Dan got me seated at the gate area and went to the desk to check in. A screaming, screeching, wailing noise broke the grim silence.

The noise got louder and louder. A woman of about thirty-five appeared, held up by two men. The noise continued, unabated.

"It's going to be a long flight if she keeps that up," Dan said.

"Maybe it would be better if I was doing that. I can't get the horror outside my body."

"Everybody does things differently," he said. "That lady's going to drive me nuts!"

The plane seemed like a cave. I shivered. The skimpy airline blanket could not keep the cold away; it was coming from the inside.

After arriving at the airport, we got on a bus. The wailing woman was in the seat behind us.

"This doesn't look like a city. Are we in Detroit?" I asked Dan.

"The crash site was not in the city. The hotel is near the crash sight."

"I don't want to see the crash site!"

"The crash site's been sealed except for emergency workers."

In the hotel room, I turned on the television. There was continuing coverage of the plane crash. The pictures of the site, taken by a helicopter, looked like the pictures I had seen of tornado damage. Bits of matter, I shuddered to think what, were strewn everywhere. Maybe Emily and Elizabeth were dazed and wandering around somewhere. The newscaster said that the young survivor was Cecilia Cichan. I had hoped against all reason that the little girl would be Elizabeth. Now there was no magic ladder out of this well of death.

Dan answered a knock at the door. An African American man, dressed in a dark blue suit, entered the room with Dan.

"This is Mr. Rivers from Northwest Airlines. He's been assigned to us."

"What do you want?" I demanded.

"I want to do anything I can for you, Ms. Weissman," he said.

He and Dan had a quiet conversation before Mr. Rivers left.

"It's almost time to go, Annie," Dan said softly.

I looked at him. His mouth was set grimly. I stood up and wrapped my sweater tighter around myself.

The people in the lobby clustered in family groups, whispering if they spoke at all. No one spoke to anyone outside their group. A white van drove up to the entrance and a group of people got out and came into the lobby. Some were crying; some had vacant stares.

Dan and I were led, with a group of others, to the van. After I was seated, I realized that Mr. Rivers was next to me.

"We're going over to the temporary morgue. You'll be asked to look at items taken from the bodies. They are all tagged. If you see something that belonged to your daughters or their father, please let me know. More and more items are being found, so this will be one of several trips."

"I don't think I would recognize any of Rob's jewelry. We haven't been together for six years," I said.

"That's okay, just take a look," Mr. Rivers replied.

Dan wiped tears from my face and put his arm around me. I hadn't realized that I was crying. He helped me from the van.

I didn't know what to expect, but the room came as a surprise. It was a hangar, enormous with no adornment. There were long folding tables set up with small items, each had a tag on it with a number. I went up to the first table and saw rings, watches, necklaces and bracelets spread out. They were oddly shaped, perhaps melted. Horror rolled over me like a huge wave and almost knocked me down in its undertow. My babies suffered and burned! I turned away and forced the thoughts from my head. Dan held my hand firmly as I walked around each table. Nothing looked familiar.

"Ready to go back Ms. Weissman?" Mr. Rivers asked.

"Yes. Please call me Annie. What happens if I can't identify anything?"

"The coroner will be checking dental records. Do you have your dentist's telephone number with you?"

"Yes, we've been going to him for fifteen years, since we moved to Phoenix. He was still Rob's dentist, too. Emily just got a full set of braces. They were laced with colored rubber bands. Elizabeth had a retainer. That should be easy to identify,"

"We need the dental records for a formal positive identification," he said. "Please call the dentist when you get back to the hotel."

My name rang out as I entered the hotel lobby. I saw Rob's sister and her husband, waving at me. They rushed over and hugged me.

"I just saw them Saturday night at my mother's house! Mother wanted me to ask you if it was all right if we had a joint funeral and burial for Rob and the girls."

I hadn't thought ahead to a funeral or burial. I was overwhelmed with the idea of making arrangements.

"I guess so," I managed to say and walked towards the elevator.

Dan and I went to our room. I lay down on the bed, trying to remember my last telephone conversation with Emily and Elizabeth. Had I told them I loved them? I couldn't be sure.

"We haven't eaten all day. Let's go downstairs and get some dinner," Dan suggested.

"I don't feel like eating, but I could use a cup of hot tea."

We rode the elevator down with the wailing woman. Her decibel level had gone down. The screams came out as guttural moans.

Dan convinced me to order a bowl of soup at the hotel restaurant. I took a few spoonfuls and pushed it aside. I cradled the hot crockery of tea in my hands, taking small sips.

Dan ordered a large meal and took his time eating it.

I saw a man dressed in a black suit with a white collar going from table to table, sitting with people. Who called him and how did he know who was here because of the crash? Then I realized that all the people staying at the hotel were connected to the crash: airline personnel, relief workers, and what the media was calling "survivors". What a strange word to use. I wasn't on the plane. I didn't survive the plane crash, watching helplessly as others perished.

The clergyman approached our table.

"May I be of assistance in your time of need?"

"Can you bring back my children?"

The clergyman had a pained and uncomfortable look on his face.

"I wanted to know if I could help you deal with your tragedy," he said.

"I'm Jewish, so I don't want to talk to a Christian minister about death and the afterlife," I said in an unfriendly tone.

"Thank you for your concern," Dan added hastily.

The man nodded and went to the next table.

"Annie, you didn't need to be nasty to him," Dan said.

"I don't want anyone butting in my life. I'm a private person and I want to stay that way." I put my hands around the mug even though it was cold and the tea was gone.

When we went up to the hotel room I called my sister to check on my parents. She offered to come to Detroit, but I didn't want to have to deal with anyone else's grief. "I don't understand why daddy had to live long enough to know about this. If he's going to die soon, he should have died before the crash.

I also called Carol and found out that the media were using school photos of my daughters and were hanging around my house.

My neighbor had promised to call in a few favors and get them to leave before I came home.

*   *   *

I couldn't sleep. I'd already awakened Dan three or four times and he held me while I cried. Now he was snoring softly.

I quietly slipped out of bed, stumbled through the darkness and found some hotel stationery. I felt my way to the bathroom, flipped on the light, and was momentarily blinded. The cold from the little white tiles went through my socks. I always wore socks to bed in the winter, and this felt like winter. I put down the lid of the toilet and sat on it. I started a poem about Elizabeth and Emily.

> "Plane Crash
>> A fire consumed my two angels.
> It snuffed out their lives
>> instantly and forever,
> But they will live on
>> in my heart . . . ."

The words flowed more freely than my tears. By three in the morning I still couldn't sleep so I called Susan.

"My God, how are you doing?"

"Not too well."

"Is there anything I can do?"

"No. There's nothing anyone can do. There's really nothing I want to say. I just wanted to hear your voice. I shouldn't have called; it's the middle of the night."

"You know you can call me anytime."

"I'm hollow. I keep hoping that Emily and Elizabeth will turn up, that they're wandering around, dazed."

"It's too much for you to handle."

"Dan's been great. He doesn't show his emotions, which seems to bother other people. For me, now, it's best because then I don't have to deal with his feelings, only mine. God, that sounds selfish."

"You're entitled to do anything that helps you through. When is the last time you slept?"

"I'm not sure. I haven't been able to sleep at all here."

"Haven't they given you some drugs? Someone should have given you some sleeping pills and tranquilizers. Tell someone tomorrow to call a doctor and get you some. There is no way you can tough this one out without help."

"I'll ask Mr. Rivers. I don't want to talk anymore."

"Anything you want to do is fine. Just know that I love you and will help you any way I can."

I hung up the receiver and looked out the hotel window to the stark light of the parking lot below. I was a stranger and didn't belong here.

* * *

Daylight finally rescued me from the long night. My head felt like someone had left me in the steam room for too long, then buried me in sand. I took a long hot shower, trying to feel my body. I used to call a student a "space case." Now I knew what it meant to be one.

I dressed in black jeans and a black shirt. Wearing black felt very right, one of the few things I was sure about these days. Dan awoke and gave me soft hug as he went into the bathroom.

I turned on the television. The morning news programs were still showing the crash sight over and over. The reporter said the crash may have been due to pilot error. I don't need to know this now, I thought. The pilot paid with his life for being human. And I will pay the rest of my life. Could it have been prevented? I swallowed the rage and it flashed thorough my body like a strike of lightning.

At breakfast Mr. Rivers joined us. I told him I wanted some drugs.

"What do you mean?" he asked, his eyes moving quickly from me to Dan and back to me.

"I haven't been able to sleep at all," I said. "I feel really weird. I don't know if it's the crash or the lack of sleep."

"I'll get in touch with a doctor but I'm sure he'll want to see you. He won't prescribe anything over the phone."

"We don't have a car to go anywhere."

"I'll take care of it. I've been talking to your family, arranging for them to come to Phoenix for the funeral. Do you know what mortuary you want?"

"Please call the rabbi at my temple," I said. "I trust whatever he says about that. Tell him I don't have the money"

"You don't have to worry about that, the airline will take care of it. When were you planning to go back to Phoenix?"

"I'll go back as soon as I've identified Emily and Elizabeth's bodies."

"Emily's body has been identified by dental records. Some of the families are going to have the bodies buried in Detroit."

"I'm taking my babies back to Phoenix. When is the next van leaving for the temporary morgue?"

"Vans leave every half hour. This is the last day the morgue will be open."

My tea had been steeping quite a while and it was very strong. I wrapped my hands around the mug as I waited for it to cool.

"Dan tells me that you want to go to Missouri to see his sons before you go back to Phoenix. I can arrange that."

The trip to the morgue in the morning was not successful.

Nothing of Elizabeth's was on display. When I went to the bathroom in the building which housed the temporary morgue, a woman in a uniform followed me. As I washed my hands, I caught the woman staring at my arms.

They're probably looking for needle tracks, I thought. They think I'm a drug addict because I asked for some sleeping pills!

I felt more desperate on the van trip over to the temporary morgue in the afternoon, my last chance to identify Elizabeth's body. I was not going to leave without doing that. Things looked almost the same as I went from table to table, but there were fewer items on the table. Relatives had identified most of them. Rob's sister had left after identifying his watch and a ring. What would be found of Elizabeth's to display? She didn't wear jewelry or a watch. I didn't see her glasses. After scrutinizing all the artifacts on all the tables, I sat down on a bench.

"I want to see the bodies, Dan. I insist on seeing the bodies. I'll know Elizabeth. Please find someone and tell them I want to see the bodies. I know they're right behind these walls."

Dan left for a moment and came back with the coroner, an older man with very bushy gray eyebrows.

"The bodies are not in good enough shape for families to view," he protested.

"I'm not leaving until I identify the body of my daughter. She was seven years old. She wasn't wearing any jewelry. Her hair was too short for a clip or ribbon. If I see the bodies I'll find her. I'm not leaving this place until I do." My pursed mouth was undermined by my trembling lips.

"Many of the bodies are not in a recognizable form. Remember there was an explosion and a fire." He looked at me with pity and sorrow.

"I will recognize her clothes."

"How old a child are we talking about?" he asked gently.

"Elizabeth is seven years old, but she's a tall girl with a baby face."

"What did she look like?"

"She has short, brown, wavy hair. She has three teeth missing and wears a retainer. She's of medium build, not thin and not fat. She has dark blue eyes."

"Maybe she was put with the older group of children's bodies. I'll go back and look for you."

"Thank you, I appreciate your time."

I turned and said to Dan, "I'm going to the bathroom, again. That's the bad part about drinking so much tea."

I noticed a relief worker, in a uniform, following me. When I went to wash my hands, the woman watched me.

"I'm not going to commit suicide by bashing my head with a toilet seat. Stop following me into the bathroom!" I shouted as I stormed out of the rest room and over to the bench where Dan sat.

"Has the coroner been back?"

"Yes, he went back to look some more."

A few minutes later, the coroner returned and sat down next to me.

"I want you to look at this lock of hair and this piece of cloth. I cut them from one of the bodies that could be your daughter."

I looked at the wet piece of hair he put in front of me. It was curling in opposite directions, so reminiscent of Elizabeth's independent and affectionate personality.

"It could be Elizabeth's. It looks a little dark, but it's wet."

"How about this material?" he asked as held it up.

"Oh my God! That's Elizabeth's! Her blue and white flowered skirt with the lace trim!"

"Are you sure?"

"It's wet, and not same color any more, but I recognize the print."

"The color would have changed in the aftermath of the crash. I'll tag the body," he said and left.

Despair engulfed me, dragging me into a whirlpool of misery and sorrow. It was really true, unalterably true. Emily and Elizabeth were dead. I allowed Dan to put his arms around me as I sobbed, gasping for breath.

When we returned to the hotel, Mr. Rivers was waiting for us in the lobby.

"Annie identified Elizabeth's body. When can we leave?" Dan asked.

"I'll make arrangements for tomorrow," Mr. Rivers said. "I'll accompany you to St. Louis, then you'll take a commuter plane to Springfield. Ms. Weissman, right now there is a doctor in room 202 seeing people."

There was a short line outside the doctor's makeshift office. When it was my turn, I sat down where the doctor indicated.

"What can I do for you?" he asked.

"I haven't been able to sleep. My daughters and ex-husband were on the plane."

"Do you have any heart or blood pressure problems or take tranquilizers?"

"No, I'm a healthy person," I replied.

"I'm going to prescribe two medications. One is a sleeping pill, the other is Valium. You can take that during the day if your anxiety level gets too high."

"How do I get the prescriptions filled?"

"Just sign this and a courier will take the prescription to the pharmacy with the others. It will be delivered to your hotel room."

The line outside the doctor's hotel room was much longer when Dan and I walked back to the elevator.

"Guess word gets around quickly here," I said.

The prescriptions arrived within an hour.

"I think I'll wait until tonight and take a sleeping pill," I said.

"It's only five o'clock," Dan said. "Why don't you take one of the other pills now? We'll watch some television, then go down to dinner."

I went into the bathroom and looked in the mirror. I was shocked at the image. The mirror had been used to comb my hair and brush my teeth, but I couldn't remember the last time I had noticed myself. My complexion was gray. Wrinkles had appeared on my cheeks and around my mouth. Pain stabbed in my jaws and clenched teeth. I put some water in a glass and took a Valium.

At dinner I still didn't feel like eating. The pill didn't seem to have made any difference. The dining room was hushed, even though every table was filled with people. That night I took a pill and sleep mercifully enveloped me.

*   *   *

Chapter 12

Pain—has an Element of Blank—
It cannot recollect
When it begun—or if there were
A time when it was not—

-Emily Dickinson

I was terrified to get on the airplane. Every time I thought about it, my heart raced and pictures of planes crashing flashed through my head. I took a Valium at breakfast, but didn't feel any calmer. I knew there was no other time effective way to go to Missouri, then Phoenix today, but I did not want to fly. A plane had betrayed my confidence and taken my babies. Yet Dan and I were taking two planes to Missouri, then two to Phoenix. Four take offs and four landings to endure. I dreaded the takeoffs most because that's when Elizabeth, Emily, and Rob's plane crashed. I wondered how much time they had suffered. I stopped and did not allow my mind to touch that subject. The coroner had said that everyone had died on impact. He probably said that whether or not it was true.

"I don't think I can get on this plane," I whispered to Dan.

"You don't have a choice," Dan said.

I accepted his statement as fact, took his outstretched hand and followed him and Mr. Rivers into the cage-like interior of the plane, my hands gripped his after we settled in our seats. I sang camp songs in my head to block out the take off procedures and announcement.

After the plane was in the air awhile, I heard Dan's voice.

"I called Diana, at her parents' home in Missouri, after you zonked out last night. She's driving Nick and Eric to my parents' house in Springfield this morning. She told the boys last week about the new living arrangements, but she wanted to know if we'd changed our minds about having the boys full time."

"I haven't." I whispered fervently. "I still love them. I still want them. And now I need them."

Mr. Rivers said his good byes at the gate of the Springfield bound airplane. He gave me his card and said I should call him if he could be of any assistance. After he left, I looked out the window.

"There's only a small plane out there, Dan."

"Yup, that's the one we're taking to Springfield."

Fear froze me.

"Dan, will you please get me a Diet Coke?"

When Dan returned with my drink, I took another Valium. I got into a plane that reminded me of the inside of a shark's belly. At least we had seats together. By the time the plane took off, the Valium kicked in and my mind was nowhere to be found.

* * *

I was with the boys when Dan gave them the news, but I sat with Dan's father in the study while Dan answered their questions about the crash.

"Annie," my father-in-law said, "I wish there was something I could do to help you. The only thing I know is law. When you're ready to think about that, let me know. I'd be glad to help you evaluate a lawyer."

"No attorney can give me what I want. I want Emily and Elizabeth alive."

"You call me when you're ready and we'll talk about it."

"I appreciate your offer."

"Grace and I will be out in Phoenix for the funeral. Let us know if there's anything we can do for you."

"Thanks, Bob."

I leaned back in the deep cushion of the rattan chair and tried not to feel so it wouldn't hurt so badly.

An hour later we were again at an airport, preparing to fly back to Phoenix. I was afraid to take another Valium, but even more terrified to get on the plane. I went to the water fountain and took a pill.

The Valium made me feel peculiar and far away. I couldn't even read during the flights. I fell asleep after the plane took off.

*   *   *

The sunshine glaring through my bedroom windows helped me figure out I was back in Phoenix. Good to be in my own bed, but I had a headache that reminded me of a hangover. Too many drugs. I was grateful I had things to do, finite things like talking to the rabbi to arrange the funeral, going to the mortuary, buying a black dress.

Dan came into the bedroom, toweling himself. "Will you be okay if I go to work today? I need to follow up some leads. I'm taking the boys with me. Let me call Carol and see if she can come over."

"I'll be okay. I don't need a babysitter. It's hard to see my friends. They were close to Emily and Elizabeth and I can't bear their grief, too. If I want company to go on my errands, I'm sure Carol will go with me."

"You're sure it's all right for me to leave you?" Dan asked as he got dressed.

"Yes, Dan, you can go to work," "and escape for a while" I muttered to myself.

I got out of bed, took a long shower, and dressed in a clean pair of dark blue jeans and a navy blue shirt since I had no more clean black clothing. I put a load of clothes in the washer and decided to buy more black pants and blouses. I sat at the kitchen table, with a cup of hot tea, to make a list of things to do. I waited until nine o'clock to call the Temple office.

"I need to make arrangements for the funeral," I said to the rabbi.

"Let me offer my condolences for your losses. Emily and Elizabeth were wonderful children. Emily did such a wonderful reading for her bat mitzvah. And Elizabeth could always be counted on for her enthusiasm during Sunday School."

"Thank you, Rabbi, for knowing and appreciating them."

"Rob's parents have already telephoned. They would like a memorial service followed by the burial. They asked if it was all right to have cameras from the television stations in the sanctuary."

I took in a short breath. "That's not what I want at all. I don't want it to become a media event. This is private."

"Annie, friends of yours and the girls have been calling us to find out the time of the service. There'll be many people attending the funeral. If you don't want the media, we know how to keep them out."

"If Rob's parents want something different, they can have a separate service."

"Annie, what I recommend is a private burial at the cemetery on Sunday morning and a memorial service at one in the afternoon in the sanctuary."

"That sounds fine, Rabbi."

"Who will be giving a speech about the girls?"

"I've been thinking about that. I wrote a poem the other night in Detroit when I couldn't sleep. I would like to read it as my final gift to my girls."

"That's up to you, if you think you can handle it. Remember, it will be a very emotional time for you. I'll ask Rob's parents who's going to say something about him. Have you spoken to the people at the Sinai Mortuary? They were told the remains would be transported to Phoenix tomorrow."

"I didn't know which mortuary. I'll call them this morning."

"Annie, if there's anything I can do for you, please don't hesitate to call."

My voice cracked as I said "Thank you" and hung up.

*   *   *

Carol and I went shopping at the Park Central Mall, close to my house, for a black dress and shoes for the funeral. It was a tough assignment for a hot Phoenix afternoon. The stores had not yet stocked the fall clothes. They were still trying to sell, at sale prices, the pastel summer clothes which Phoenicians would wear for another two and a half months until it cooled down in October.

I usually loved to shop but today my clothes weighed hundreds of pounds as I took them off to try on yet another black dress. Finally I compromised and bought a suitable one made of a black crepe material that skimmed my body and had a round white collar. On the way out of the store, I saw some black blouses and bought three.

"Don't you think three is a bit excessive?" Carol ventured.

"No. I can't bear to wear any colors but black and navy blue. I'll probably go shopping for black clothes for work."

"When does the school year start?"

"Teachers go back next week. Students start the week after."

"Are you going to take some time off?" Carol asked.

"No, I won't feel better wandering around the rooms at home alone."

"Where do you want to go for shoes?"

"I'm done in. I'll postpone the search for the shoes until tomorrow. Susan should be here by then. Let's get a cup of tea."

We went over to the delicatessen in the mall. I ate half of a bowl of chicken soup and some tea. Even though the weather outside was steamy (110 degrees and 40% humidity), the hot tea soothed me and warmed my body, grown cold and numb with pain.

"You seem to be too calm, Annie. I know you're a strong person, but I don't think you're letting enough out."

"I can't," I said. "It's too big and scary. Anytime I start to feel it, my heart literally feels like it's being stabbed over and over again. I cry in the middle of the night. Dan's been wonderful. He just holds me."

"We're all here for you, Annie. You only have to give us a sign."

"There's really nothing anyone can do for me. I shouldn't say that. I appreciate all you've done with the calls to everyone. I'm tired. I want to go home and rest."

"Sure, Annie."

Carol dropped me off at my house. I brought in the mail, mostly cards, probably sympathy cards. I didn't open them.

I went into my bedroom and took out the poem I'd written in

Detroit. I read a few lines. The paper fell from my hands. I threw myself down on the bed and cried myself to sleep.

The jangling phone harshly woke me, a brutal return to consciousness. I was nonplused to hear my former sister-in-law's voice.

"I'm calling for my mother. She talked to the rabbi about the memorial service arrangements and she's very upset. She had it all worked out and you changed everything."

"I made the decisions about the burial and services for Emily and Elizabeth. If your mother wants something different for Rob, she can do what she pleases by setting his service at another time."

"Our family definitely wants to have one service for the three of them. We also want the television cameras there. Rob was well respected with a certain position in this city."

"I will choose how and when my daughters will be buried."

"Mother also wants to know about who you're getting to cater the reception after the service. We assumed it would be at your house since it's so close to the temple."

"My friends arranged a reception at my next door neighbor's house. They're providing the food. You can have a reception anywhere you like if you want to make it fancy. Everyone is welcome at my reception, whether they came to the service for Rob or the girls."

"Annie, you are being an uncooperative bitch!"

"I don't want to talk to you any more."

I slammed down the phone. Anger energized me. I paced the dark blue rug in the bedroom, ranting aloud.

"Witch! You criticized me when I was married to Rob. You're still being nasty! You bitch! You want a big show! Forget it! I want a simple, respectful funeral, not a circus! This time I'm getting my way!

As soon as I said the word "funeral", the anger evaporated, leaving the sorrow uncovered, as the dew leaves the grass a victim to the August sun.

*　　*　　*

On the day of the burial and memorial service, I was groggy even after a long hot, then cool shower. Probably the sleeping pills. I took them every night but refrained from taking the Valium during the day because I was scared that I'd get addicted. Pills would be an easy way to put off ever feeling the pain.

Dan was busy getting Nick and Eric showered, dressed, and breakfasted. I worried about the effect Emily's and Elizabeth's deaths would have on them. I was lucky the boys were living with us. It gave me a reason not to crumble into dust. They needed me. Their hugs and kisses sustained me more than food. I held on to the "mother" part of my identity.

I dressed but didn't put on makeup. It would only run when I cried. I put on the new dark prescription sunglasses. They shielded my vulnerability. As I was fluffing my hair, I noticed the pill bottles. I took a Valium, allowing myself help to get through the day.

The mortuary limousine drove us out to the Temple cemetery. I'd never been there and imagined a picturesque thick carpet of grass with huge shade trees. The cemetery was in an industrial area just west of downtown. Grass had a hard time taking hold, resulting in bare patches of ground that formed a crazy quilt. There was a white plastic ramada on wheels that shaded the burial area. When I got out of the limousine, the hot, arid air took my breath away.

When I walked closer to the ramada, I could see the gaping holes in the earth and the three caskets. I shuddered at the unalterable proof that Emily, Elizabeth, and Rob were dead. Their bodies had been cremated, unusual for Jews, but the mortician said it was due to the "state of the remains". A picture of Elizabeth and Emily screaming, covered with flames, jumped into my head but I banished it with a silent scream.

There were about forty people gathered under the ramada as I'd only told family and good friends about the burial. Rob's family was already there. I took a seat next to my mother and sister.

The rabbi was speaking but I couldn't pay attention to what he was saying. My mind was fixed on the holes in the ground. Dan nudged me when it was time to put flowers on the caskets in the holes: pink roses for Emily and white calla lilies for Elizabeth. The rabbi said some more things but sorrow deafened me. When Dan stood up I realized the ceremony was over.

I hugged my mother, sister, and brother, then went to Rob's father. I'd always gotten along with him. He gave me a hug. No one else in the family approached, so I turned away. Each of my friends gave me a firm hug as I walked back towards the car.

The ride home was silent. There was an hour before the memorial service. Susan brought in lunch for Dan and the boys but I couldn't eat. I sought comfort in hot tea as the outside temperature climbed towards 115. I excused myself and went into the bathroom to take another Valium, then sat down on my bed to go over my short speech

Susan came in and sat next to me, putting her arms around me.

"I know this is a terrible day. My heart aches for you. I'm worried I'll say or do the wrong thing."

"I always felt that way, too, when someone had a death in the family. Now I know there are very few wrongs things to say, only that nothing makes you feel better, so it doesn't much matter what's said."

Dan poked his head in and announced it was time to leave.

We loaded up the stretch van and drove the mile to the Temple.

The streets were lined with cars, but no television vans. Dan and Susan took the boys into the sanctuary. The rabbi led me to his study to wait for the service to begin. He was a bald old man who usually had a smile on his face. Today, he was solemn in his white robe and prayer shawl. The fringes of his prayer shawl fluttered on the waves of the air conditioning.

"It's time for us to join the others," the rabbi said as he gently put his hand on the small of my back, helped me up, walked me to the sanctuary, and guided me onto the platform. I saw an ocean of faces in the pews but couldn't distinguish who was who. I sat on the *bimah*, a bench behind the rabbi, shielding myself from everyone in the pews.

The rabbi began the service. I tuned in and out.

"Blessed is the Lord our God Ruler of the Universe . . . "

El Male Rachamin, the prayer asking for a perfect rest for the dead, consoled me.

The rabbi nodded at me. I walked slowly to the lectern.

"Rob and I had many happy years together. Our paths diverged and we went our separate ways. My family narrowed to Emily and Elizabeth. They were the lights of my life.

"Some of the times were tough but supportive friends were always there, our safety net. I thank all of you now for the special and ordinary things you did for Emily and Elizabeth.

"I gave them what I couldn't afford: religious training, acting school, musical instruments with private lessons, the best child care, clothes and toys they didn't need but wanted, a bat mitzvah party, and any Halloween costumes we could dream up. I also gave them time, lots of time and energy. I thank God now that I did. There are no regrets.

"I know Emily and Elizabeth treasured the time spent with their friends, grandparents, aunts, uncles, and cousins. I want to thank my parents for their love and many-faceted support. The girls were very concerned about Grandpa Ben's illness and expected daily reports.

"This past year Emily and Elizabeth had a new family: two brothers, Nick and Eric; and a stepfather, Dan. The family spirit was there from the first weekend we spent at the cabin in Pinetop. The affection grew fast and deep. They treated each other as brothers and sisters. Eric and Elizabeth took to calling each other 'twin'. Emily and Elizabeth grew to accept Dan as another father, not one to replace Rob, whom they loved dearly, but as a parent who could be counted on to plan excursions and bring fun into every day life, to lighten up the household, to attend the concerts, plays, swim meets, and T ball games.

"I'm an optimist. My philosophy of life is to do my best, expect it of others, and look for the good side of every situation. Emily and Elizabeth shared this philosophy. It is very difficult to do that now, but I wrote this poem in that spirit."

The tears ran silently down my face as I read.

"Plane Crash
A fire consumed my two angels.
It snuffed out their lives
        instantly and forever,
But they will live on
        in our hearts.
Emily was my sunshine

poised
brilliant
caring
sensitive
a brave heart
loyal friend
loving sister
an almost too perfect child.
Elizabeth was my rainbow
light-hearted
open
friendly
vibrant
a rascal
cheerful
loving sister
an endearing child.
They were both good hearted people
beautiful
loving
imaginative.
They made a positive difference to all
who knew them.
I miss my angels but take heart that
they knew no deep sorrows
no broken dreams
no betrayal
no war, hunger or personal violence.
They led short but charmed lives
yet felt for others.
It is for us, the living,
to remember their happy lives
And know they are with God.
Think not of the future, unfulfilled
but of the happy lives they led."

I looked at the audience. I saw Carol, tears streaming down her face. Emily's friends Rachel and Amanda were clinging to their mothers and sobbing. Dan had an arm around each of his boys. I walked unsteadily back to my seat.

Rob's brother gave the eulogy for him. It was short but I didn't listen. My mind was a blender, thoughts whirling incomprehensibly. I heard the rabbi close with the *Kaddish,* the prayer which glorifies God. My parents were atheists who believed that it's all over when you die. I couldn't believe that, especially now. I wanted to think that Emily's and Elizabeth's souls were with God. God couldn't control the world, because I couldn't comprehend God had a purposeful hand in their deaths.

During the reception at Karlene's home, it was hard to concentrate on what people said. Many people from school were there, even the superintendent. My principal said she would do anything she could to make things easier for me.

The most painful was to see Emily and Elizabeth's friends. They were hurting but they were alive.

Later that evening, after the children were put to bed and relatives sent back to their hotels, Carol, Susan, and I sat around my kitchen table. Carol and Susan were sharing a bottle of wine. A cup of hot tea warmed my hands.

"Sure you don't want to smoke a joint?" Susan asked. "Harvey sent one for you."

"No, drugs won't help," I said. "I've already taken two Valium today and I've been taking sleeping pills at night. I'm so far down there is no up. I'm living a bad dream and I'm afraid of what will happen when the shock wears off. "

"I grieve for Emily and Elizabeth, but my heart is breaking for you," said Susan.

"I can't handle anyone else's grief," I said. "That's why it's so hard to be with you."

"We'll say or do anything you want, Annie", said Carol.

"What I want can never be again. Lose me in the past. Tell me stories."

We were silent for a minute.

Susan started. "Do you remember when you and Rob came to visit me in San Francisco when Emily was two months old? We drove to Tiburon. On the way back we stopped at a Safeway to pick up groceries. Rob tossed Emily in the air to hear her belly laugh. You warned him not to do that. In the middle of the Safeway, he tossed her in the air again and Emily spit up all over him."

The story evinced a small laugh from me.

"I remember one Sunday afternoon, after you and Rob had separated, you came over with Elizabeth and Emily for a barbecue," Carol said. "Elizabeth went inside to go to the bathroom. When she was gone for more than five minutes, you went looking for her and found her in front of my stereo. She had broken off the diamond needle of the phonograph and was trying to dismantle the speakers. You insisted on replacing the needle even though you were broke because Rob had cleaned out your bank accounts. You were so relieved to find the needle for $10.00 on a closeout sale. That Elizabeth was always into mischief!"

"I remember all the singing you and Emily did the summer you stayed with me in San Francisco," Susan said. "The two of you memorized all the words on the 'Bert and Ernie Sing Along' tape and Elizabeth would clap her hands to the music."

Carol added, "Remember when Emily was first learning to talk at Christmas time? She must have been eighteen months old. She couldn't say 'duck'. It came out sounding like 'fuck'. We took the kids to see the Disney decorations at Metrocenter. She got very excited and yelled several times at the top of her lungs, 'Look Mommy, Donald Fuck!' We laughed until we peed in our pants."

"One time when I was visiting you in Phoenix," Susan said. "I took Emily out shopping. Somehow we started talking about singing voices. Emily described your voice, when you used to sing to her at bedtime, as the best voice that couldn't carry a tune. She thought her vocal talent had come from another generation, since Rob rasped more than sang."

"The stories bring back good memories," I said with a hiccup as I brushed away some tears. "Thanks, I love you two!"

We all hugged. I finally pulled away and said, "I'm ready to call it a night."

I showed them to the door, took a sleeping pill, and welcomed oblivion.

*　　*　　*

CHAPTER 13

Icicles upon my soul
Prickled Blue and Cool—

-Emily Dickinson

The next morning, life went on. People returned to their lives, flying home or going back to work. And there I was, drinking hot tea in my house, overwhelmed by memories. Nick and Eric were in the family room watching cartoons. At least Carol and Susan were still around. Susan had decided to stay an extra two days and Carol took a few vacation days from work.

Susan and Carol wanted to clean out Emily and Elizabeth's rooms. I needed to go in and put in a pile those things I wanted to keep. They would pack them and put the boxes into the garage. They would get rid of everything else.

I couldn't go in my daughters' rooms. I wasn't ready for all vestiges of their existence to disappear.

I made myself take a shower and get dressed. I managed to remove Nick and Eric from the grip of the television long enough for them to shower and dress. I tried to read an Agatha Christie book, but I couldn't focus long enough to understand how the individual sentences fit together, let alone remember which character was which.

Susan showed up at my door first, dressed in an old tee shirt and shorts, with a San Francisco Giants baseball cap on her head. She was holding several boxes, obviously ready to start clearing things out.

"I'm not prepared for this," I protested.

"I know it's soon, but you need to be practical. Nick and Eric are still sleeping in the bunk beds in the back room. They need to move into Emily and Elizabeth's rooms. You can't ask them to live with Emily and Elizabeth's things."

"I know but I can't bear it, that's all," I said with an edge to my voice. "I haven't been in their rooms since the crash.

Susan took my hand and led me to Emily's "Peach Palace." The curtains were peach, the comforter was peach, even the sheets were peach.

"I know you want to keep the pictures, especially the prints of my work," Susan said in an obvious effort to lighten the moment.

I went around the room picking up school reports, papers, photos, jewelry, and drawings. I looked in the closet but didn't take anything out.

We went into Elizabeth's "Rainbow Room". I clutched the well-worn Curious George stuffed monkey that Elizabeth had hugged and loved. I finally tucked Curious George under my arm, gathered up a few drawings and a T ball trophy from the room, and hurried back to the relative safety of the living room.

Carol arrived with more boxes.

"Save all the books," I said. "I'll want them for the boys or students at school."

"I think it would be a good idea if you went out with Nick and Eric for a few hours. We'll move the boys' things into the rooms and meet you for lunch somewhere."

"I guess I can take them to the park. We could meet for lunch at Hamburger Works."

"That sounds fine," Carol said.

I went into the family room to talk to Nick and Eric. "We're going to go over to the park," I said, "and you can feed the ducks."

"Do we have to?" asked Nick.

I missed Emily and Elizabeth. They were always willing to go anywhere with me.

"We'll have fun. Turn off the TV and get your shoes and socks on."

"Okay," they sighed.

While they were searching for their shoes, I said to Carol, "I have a favor to ask, Carol. Paco needs to get his books and stuff at the high school and I can't handle it. Would you take care of it? It's complicated because he has several scholarships for the bookstore."

"Sure, no problem."

"Would you also see a counselor or whoever is in charge of the at-risk program? Paco needs to be targeted for immediate monitoring."

"I'll make sure he's taken care of, Annie. I'm glad you finally asked me to do something. Where's Paco now?"

"He's at home. I was going to pick him up."

"How about if I fetch him? I know where he lives since I drove him to the funeral."

"That would be great, Carol. I feel so guilty that I can't be there for him."

"You have to take care of yourself, Annie. I like the kid! It's no problem."

I remembered bread for the ducks, the same ducks that scared Elizabeth into my arms when she was two years old. Nick, Eric, and I went to the park but no one was in a mood to play.

*   *   *

The next morning, armed with Nick and Eric's birth certificates and shot records, I drove to Encanto Elementary School to register them. I wavered at the entrance of the red brick office I had frequented so many times with Emily and Elizabeth.

Inside, I met Mrs. Pogue, Elizabeth's teacher from last year. She hugged me and told me what a wonderful girl Elizabeth was. She wanted Eric in her class. I readily agreed, knowing her to be a kind and effective teacher.

I asked the school secretary to choose a teacher for Nick, someone understanding to keep Nick's self esteem intact. The secretary recommended a fifth grade teacher who always had a kind word for everyone.

I spent an hour writing out formal requests for the teachers, filling out registration forms, and after school care forms. I got a map of the school with Mrs. Pogue's and Mr. Bailey's rooms circled so Dan could find them on the first day.

I was exhausted when I arrived at my own school.

Almost everyone on the staff stopped by sometime that week to give me a hug and see how I was doing. I knew they all meant well, but I wanted to be able to lose myself at school.

By Friday afternoon the library was ready. I felt the excitement that always came with the start of a new school year. I looked forward to settling into a comfortable routine. I had a bottle of Valium in my purse, as back up, but I hadn't used it for the past few days. I took a sleeping pill every other night.

On the way home from school I stopped by Paco's apartment. I hadn't heard from him since the funeral. I wanted to make sure everything was okay for him to start high school on Monday. The best way to do that was to have him stay at my house.

I kicked a few beer cans aside in the patio and knocked at the door. The television was blasting so I pounded on the door.

Veronica, Paco's younger sister, opened it a crack. She smiled when she saw me and invited me inside.

There were people on the floor sleeping though the roar of cartoons. I made the mistake of breathing though my nose and gagged at the odorous combination of vomit and feces. Diapers and dirty dishes were strewn around the stained linoleum floor. I glanced at the three toddlers transfixed by Looney Tunes. It was impossible to guess their gender. All were wearing only disposable diapers and had dark brown, matted hair.

How unfair that these alcoholic and drug addicted teenagers get to bring up and ruin these perfectly good children while my own babies were gone. I wanted to snatch the three children and take them home.

"Paco is asleep upstairs," Veronica volunteered.

"Please wake him and tell him I'm here."

She disappeared for a minute, then told me he'd be down soon.

"Are you looking forward to school starting, Veronica?"

Her eyes lit up and she flashed a toothy grin.

"I love school," she said. "I'm going to be in the fourth grade."

"Fourth grade is fantastic," I said. "You go on field trips to the Heard Museum, Pueblo Grande, South Mountain Park, and the desert exhibit at the zoo. You're very smart, so I know you'll enjoy reading the fourth grade novels. You're welcome to visit me after school."

Paco finally stumbled down the stairs. He was wearing blue jeans shorts and a filthy white tee shirt. His eyes were red.

"What're you doing here?" he asked.

"Please spend the weekend with me, Paco. We'll get some school clothes and I can drive you for your first day of high school."

"I kinda have plans with my girlfriend. There's a big party on Saturday night."

"How about if I pick you up on Sunday afternoon?"

"I don't know where I'll be."

I strode across the room and took Paco's face in my hands.

"Do you want to go to high school and college and be a lawyer or have this future?" I pointed to the bodies on the floor.

"I'll call you on Sunday and tell you where to pick me up."

I couldn't let go of his face.

"Paco, life is not fair, believe me, I know. This is a whirlpool, dragging you down. I want it for you with my soul but you have to do it for yourself. You can do it. You're brilliant. You can live with us. Come with me now."

"I can't," he said. "I'll call you Sunday."

He loosened my grip and went back upstairs.

I went back to my car and pounded the searingly hot steering wheel. I sat in the oven of a car as punishment for not convincing Paco to come with me. As I started the engine and the air conditioning, I shouted, "You'd better call me Sunday!"

* * *

On Sunday the boys went with Dan while I watched old movies and waited for Paco to call. I ate a whole bag of m & m's and felt nauseous.

He finally called at four and gave me directions to his grandfather's house. He was waiting outside when I pulled up.

His eyes were clear and he was smiling.

"If we hurry, we can make it to Penney's before it closes," I said.

It felt good to be buying back-to-school clothes and supplies. Dan went shopping with the boys the week before, without me. Still, I wanted to be buying plaid skirts and white blouses, pink shorts, and hair ribbons.

When we returned to my house I made up the bottom bunk for Paco while he laid out his clothes and backpack on the top bunk.

I hugged him and then held him at arm's length and looked him in the eyes.

"You can do this, Paco, for yourself. You can be anything but you'll have to commit everything to the effort."

I hugged him again.

The next morning was hectic. Dan left early with Nick and Eric to take them to their new classrooms. I dropped Paco at North High and drove to my school.

I was confident as I walked out of the office. I hadn't slept well, but I never did the night before school started. Tanya, a student, ran to me and threw her arms around my hips and said, "I'm sorry your daughters died."

I croaked out, "Thank you."

As I walked down the sidewalk the scene was repeated with four more students. My breathing got shallower with each encounter. I ran into Lisa's classroom, closed the door, and leaned against it.

"My God, Annie, what's the matter?" Lisa asked. "You look ghastly!"

"All the kids know about Emily and Elizabeth. They're coming up to me on the sidewalk and saying they're sorry. I can't take it!"

Lisa got a box of tissues from her desk and gave them to me.

"Let me think about this," she said.

I went over to the sink and took a Valium with shaking hands.

"Go through the connecting doors to the library. I'll write a memo for the principal to put out by morning recess, explaining to the kids that you appreciate their sympathy but that you would rather they write you a note because it's difficult for you to talk about it."

I escaped to my library. I needed time alone to collect myself. I doubled over the sink.

Guess I wasn't doing as well as I thought.

*   *   *

CHAPTER 14

One need not be a Chamber—to be Haunted

-Emily Dickinson

Paco stayed with us until Friday. On Wednesday evening he asked me to take him for a physical for freshman football.

"I'm afraid you'll get hurt, Paco. I couldn't bear that. But if you want to play, you can get the form filled out at the county hospital, where you take your mother.

Paco shrugged.

*   *   *

When Paco didn't come back or call on Sunday, I was frantic.

"He's got to do it," Dan said. "It's so much easier for him to stay home, drink, and do drugs. You're fighting a losing battle."

"Paco is not giving up!" I screamed.

Dan put up his hands.

*   *   *

Paco came back to us on Tuesday but he went home Thursday. Then he didn't come back at all. The head of the International Baccalaureate Program called me to inquire about Paco. I had to honestly tell him that I didn't know where he was.

*   *   *

Every day was a chore. I dragged myself to school and put on my public mask. All I wanted to do at night was have a family meal then space out watching television. I could no longer lose myself in a book because I couldn't concentrate enough to read.

One Tuesday evening when Nick and Eric were with their mother, Dan asked me to go to Durant's for dinner with him and Slimebucket. I didn't want to go but Dan had asked so little of me in the past month I felt obligated.

We parked in the back lot and entered the restaurant the usual way, through the kitchen. Slimebucket already occupied a large booth. I deflated as I slumped into the padded leather bench.

Slimebucket ordered another drink. How many had he already consumed? Dan ordered a Stolee and cranberry juice and I had hot tea.

They told amusing stories about customers and contracts. I was content to listen to their complaints about the owners of the roofing company.

Slimebucket and Dan chomped on thick steaks while I ate liver and onions.

As the waitress delivered their after dinner drinks and the check, I thought the ordeal was nearly over and it hadn't been so bad.

"Annie," Slimebucket purred. "Dan and I are the key to the success of the roofing company."

"I'm sure you're both great salesmen," I said.

"We should open our own company and build our own futures," he said.

"Why?" I asked. "You both make good money and don't take on the risks or headaches."

"We won't make that kind of money for long. As soon as the owners realize how much we sell and how much we get paid, they'll change the rules of the commissions. Besides, the company's mismanaged. We need to leave before it folds."

"I can't take on anything more," I said.

"I'm not talking about this month," Slimebucket replied. "You won't get the money for a while anyway."

"Money? What are you talking about?"

"I know a shark of a lawyer who can get you a couple of million dollars from the airlines," Slimebucket said. We'd only need $100,000 to start our roofing company.

I stared at Slimebucket and tasted bile in my throat.

"You are the most despicable person I have ever met!"

I walked out of the dining room, through the kitchen, and outside. I was shaking with anger and disgust. What claim did Slimebucket have on any money from the death of my daughters?

Dan came out a minute later.

"I'm sorry," he said. He said he wanted to have dinner with you to express his sympathy. I had no idea he was going to spring that on you."

"Have you been plotting behind my back to use my settlement money?"

"No," Dan answered. "We've been talking about starting a company since I began working with him."

"I don't ever want to see that Slimebucket again!"

"I promise to bring you two together as little as possible."

We drove the short distance home in a tense silence. I took solace in a sleeping pill.

*   *   *

Two weeks later, Dan and I were in Dee's coffee shop for breakfast.

"Have you thought about when you're going to see a counselor?" Dan asked.

"I've been reading the books on grief I checked out of the library. I think I'm doing okay."

"Annie, you know I am not big on this psychology stuff, but I think you should consider seeing someone."

"I'm not sure it's time yet."

"Annie, trust me, it's time."

I studied Dan's face. Worry clouded his eyes.

"I heard there's a support group at a Catholic Church for people who lost a family member in the plane crash," Dan said.

"I don't think I'd do well in a group. I'd help other people rather than talk about myself. Carol gave me the name of someone who specializes in grief counseling. I'll call her tomorrow and set up an appointment. I have plenty of sick leave."

"I told Mr. Rivers from Northwest Airlines that you wanted to meet with the airlines' lawyers about a settlement. He gave me the number of the guy to call. I called him explained who you were and what you wanted. He jumped on the idea and wants to come to Phoenix to discuss it. He'll let me know the details of where and when."

"I appreciate you doing all the groundwork. The telephone conversation with your father really helped."

"Are you sure you want to do this yourself?"

"I'm not doing it myself, you and your dad are helping me. Dan, they know they owe me. I may need counseling the rest of my life. I don't have the money for that. What if I get depressed and can't work? We may have to move. I get the willies when I'm in the house by myself. It's filled with ghosts and memories that assault me when I'm not ready."

Dan took my hand and squeezed it.

"I know some of the families are suing together but I'm not going to join them," I said. "I don't need to wring every last dime I can get. I want to get it over with so I can go on with my life."

"If that's what you want, it's okay with me."

We finished eating silently, each immersed in worry.

*   *   *

I sat in the empty waiting room of the counselor's office.

There was no receptionist and I was fifteen minutes early for my first appointment. I couldn't focus my eyes on the *Newsweek* magazine in front of me. I wasn't sure what to expect. At precisely eight a.m. the grief counselor appeared, wearing a long green skirt, a black top and love beads. She greeted me and invited me to have a seat in her office. Three black leather chairs were gathered around a chrome and glass table.

She was silent as I sat down and filled out a form.

"Why have you come to see me?" she asked.

"My daughters and ex-husband were killed in the plane crash outside Detroit. I feel isolated and I can't let out my grief."

"Is there anyone left in your family?"

The phrasing of the question struck me as odd.

"I live with my second husband and his two sons. We got custody of them a few weeks before the crash."

"Do you think your daughters died because you took in your husband's children?"

The question socked me in the face.

"I told you my daughters died in a plane crash."

"Are you angry with your stepsons for being alive?" the counselor asked.

"What are you talking about?"

"Who do you blame for your daughters' deaths?"

"I don't know. The pilot made a mistake, but he didn't do it on purpose. The airline didn't plan the crash." I could hear the belligerence in my voice. Each of the counselor's questions seemed more absurd.

At the end of the session, I made another appointment for the same time the next week, even though I didn't feel connected to the therapist. Hell, I didn't feel connected to anyone anymore.

*   *   *

I arrived early again the next week for my counseling session. As I sat in the waiting room, there was a familiar odor. I sniffed in three times to pinpoint the smell. Marijuana smoke! Was I so depressing the counselor had to smoke a joint to deal with me?

When the grief counselor appeared, I looked into her eyes and recognized the tell tale signs of a buzz. I followed her and crouched in the chair, awaiting the onslaught of questions.

"Have you been able to discuss your anger with your stepsons?"

"I'm not angry with my stepsons."

"Are you able to enjoy sex with your husband?"

I gave the counselor one of the looks I used to silence students who insulted others.

"I am not here to discuss my sex life. Your questions last week and this week aren't helpful or relevant. You are not the right counselor for me."

Without giving her a chance to respond, I got up and strode out. I ran to my car and locked the doors. I started the engine, put the radio at its highest volume and screamed, "You bitch!" at the top of my lungs five times before I started to laugh wildly. I might be crazy, but that counselor was crazier still.

I drove home and called a counselor I had seen eight years before, when there were problems in my marriage to Rob. She might not be an expert in grief counseling, but I trusted her not to ask those horrible questions.

*   *   *

The mother of one of Emily's friends asked me to meet her for a drink after work one day, at an uptown bar that imitated the plant bars in San Francisco. She made sympathetic noises when I arrived. We both had glasses of the house white wine.

She kept going on and on about what her daughter was doing these days: school dances, being an aide at the Temple Sunday School, and Student Council elections. With each sentence, I got angrier and angrier, but I couldn't get out the words to tell her to shut up. I didn't want to hear about things Emily would have been doing! I smiled and nodded and said, "That's great!" where appropriate. Total disconnection. I never agreed to see her again.

*   *   *

October 18, 1987

Dear Emily,

I'm down in the dumps again, even lower that that. I have a tight feeling in my throat and a few tears sneak out but I haven't been able to have a good cry lately. The idea to write you a letter just popped into my head as I was fixing myself a peanut butter sandwich and brewing up a pot of tea. Perhaps it means that I am losing my mind, going further from reality. All I know is how much I miss you and Elizabeth.

I found Elizabeth's purple eyeglasses in a bag. Didn't she take them to Ohio? Or were they a pair she lost? I must be crazy. I'm asking a dead person to answer questions. I also found a small tortoise shell pair, hers or yours? I know that I should have taken them to work and let a child use the frames, but I couldn't bear to see another child wearing your glasses. I threw them in the trash in my room, but they called to me. I had Nick take the trash out to the alley yesterday but it didn't exorcise the glasses from my mind.

You were the best kids I've ever met. It is not fair that you didn't live to enjoy the rest of your lives. I saw a movie the other day, *My Life as a Dog*. I thought it would be a comedy, but it was about a boy's adjustment to his mother's illness and death. The line in the movie that I heard loudest was "It's hardest for those left behind." I do wish that I, not your dad, had been on the plane. I would have been with you at the time you needed me the most and I wouldn't have to bear life without you.

I'm glad we had five years with the three of us together, just you and me and Elizabeth. I knew a closeness with the two of you that I will never know with anyone else. I'm not forgetting the hard times, but we hung together and held each other tightly, knowing that as long as we were together, everything was okay. My world is not okay anymore because you're not with me. I sure hope you're with God, because it's unendurable to think that there is nothing more for you. I'd do anything to be able to see you and have you here again, but I'm not crazy enough to think that will happen. I went to Yiskor services at the Temple. Dan went with me. But going to the Temple is bittersweet. It brings back all the happy memories of children's services, your bat mitzvah, and yours and Elizabeth's consecrations. But the sanctuary seems to echo your absence.

Love,
Mommy

*　　*　　*

CHAPTER 15

I never lost as much but twice,
And that was in the sod.
Twice have I stood a beggar
Before the door of God!

Angels—twice descending,
Reimbursed my store—
Burglar! Banker—father!
I am poor once more!

-Emily Dickinson

On a cool evening in mid October, Dan and I drove to a rendezvous at a motel with the attorney from the airlines.

The attorney was a man in his forties and dressed in a dark blue suit, white shirt, and a red tie. He led us to his sterile room.

We seated ourselves at a round table.

"First of all, let me express my condolences for your loss," he said.

As he spoke, I noticed that he was nervously tugging on his tie with his index finger and thumb.

"Thank you," I said softly.

"We are contacting the families of the victims of the flight who have not engaged an attorney to get an idea on how they want to proceed."

"My wife would like to deal with the airlines or their insurance company directly," Dan said. "She doesn't want a lawyer making money from the death of her children. She'll have an Arizona attorney check the final agreement."

"What kind of agreement were you contemplating?"

"We don't need to beat around the bush," I said. "I want my daughters back. If I could have that, I would be the world's happiest person. But no one can give me that. I don't care to get involved in a suit and have it drag on for years. You owe me and you know it. Emily and Elizabeth were my only biological children. I had a hysterectomy so I can't have any more children." I stopped talking so I wouldn't break down crying.

"I am authorized to discuss a financial settlement on behalf of all parties concerned," he said as he started to play with his tie again.

"I haven't thought in dollar amounts. I need some money to pay for the counseling I'm getting now. I'll need some money in a lump sum to help us move because it's too difficult for me to live in my house now." I could hear the quiver in my voice and stopped to regain my composure.

"It's been a very hard for me, with some days better than others. I get worried that I won't be emotionally stable enough to do my job so I want a structured settlement where most of the money is paid on a monthly basis for a long period of time."

"Please send the counseling bills to Mr.Rivers, your liaison from the airlines. He'll see they're paid until we come to an agreement. Do you have a settlement amount in mind?"

"No," I said. "I thought I would let you go back to your office and think about it. When you come up with an offer, we can meet again and see if it's acceptable."

"Can you give me an idea of what would be a ballpark number?"

"I refuse to be the one to put a dollar amount on the worth of my children's lives."

I knew I couldn't say another word without breaking down. I looked at Dan and saw that he knew it too.

"My wife is a very strong person, but this tragedy has been almost unbearable for her. We need to leave now. Please call me when you are ready to talk again. Thank you for your time." He reached across the table and shook the attorney's hand.

Dan stood by my chair as I got up.

"I'll be calling you," the attorney said as he saw us to the door.

Dan and I walked down the sidewalk past a turn. I stopped and leaned against the wall.

"You okay?" Dan asked.

"Yeah, give me a minute," I said, gasping for air.

Dan put his arm around me.

"Are you sure you want to handle this without a lawyer?"

"Yes," I said as I started walking down the sidewalk again. "It will be over sooner if we do it ourselves. And I don't think that attorney is going to get in my face and play mean like he might to another lawyer."

The drive home took twenty-five minutes. Our neighbor Karlene had stayed with the boys. I thanked her while Dan went in to kiss the boys good night.

Dan and I met in the kitchen. He served himself a large bowl of Captain Crunch with chocolate milk while I went straight for the Milky Ways.

"Dan, what do you think about adopting a baby?"

"I was wondering how long it would take before the subject came up."

"A child wouldn't replace Emily and Elizabeth. There will never be anyone like them. We have Eric and Nick, but it isn't the same. I'm a step mom and I'll always be number three with them. You're first, Diana is second, and I'm a distant third. I don't want to interfere with how they feel about their mother or take her place."

"Nick and Eric love you, Annie."

"I know they care for me. But sometimes, when you're a little late, I get very upset. If something happens to you, the boys would go to live with Diana. And I would have no family at all."

"Don't you want to know how I feel about adopting a child?"

"Of course."

"It would be fine. I'd rather not get a baby and go through that again. I'm not very good with babies."

"It's probably too soon to do anything, but I'm thirty-nine years old. I wonder if there is a ceiling on how old you can be?"

"Let's wait a few months while you see the new counselor."

I slept fitfully that night and was drained when my alarm rang the next morning. As I was driving to school over the Seventh Avenue Salt

River bridge, I felt a deep urge to steer the car over the edge. There were just rocks in the dry riverbed. No one else would get hurt. Nick and Eric's faces flashed in my mind and I kept driving to work. I took a Valium and showed sound filmstrips the entire day.

*   *   *

I ran into my house and caught the phone on the fifth ring. "Hello," I said breathlessly.

"Hi, Annie, this is Evvy. You need to come East, Daddy died this morning."

. . . .

"Annie, are you there?"

"Yeah, I'm here."

"Annie, he was suffering. It was terrible to watch."

"I know. I just talked to him this morning. It was hard to hear his voice."

"He didn't want a funeral, but Mom wants a memorial service. He's being cremated. How soon can you come?"

"I'll get a flight out tomorrow."

I hung up the phone, slid into the nearest kitchen chair, folded my arms on the table, and put my head down. He's gone, but not soon enough. Why did he have to live long enough to feel the pain of Elizabeth and Emily's deaths? I remained in the same position for a long time, trying not to move, feel or think.

"What's going on?" Dan asked as he came in the back door and saw me.

"My father died today. I have to leave tomorrow."

"Do you want me to go with you?" he asked.

I said "no," but I wanted him to protest and insist he go. He didn't. I called and made the plane reservations. Getting on another God damned plane! When I called Carol and Susan, they offered to accompany me. I turned them down, but Susan insisted she had to go for herself. She was close to my father.

In the end, Susan and I arranged the reception at my sister's home. I spoke for the family at the service. Many of my father's friends and colleagues made remarks for the service that gave me a fuller picture of the man I thought I knew so well. I couldn't feel the total pain of my father dying; it was just too much. Parents should die before their children. It is the natural order of the world. It's sad, but expected, as they grow older. Even if it's early and an accident, parents are supposed to die first. My life was upside down. My children died before me and now my father died before me too. The laws of nature were working against me.

All my aunts and uncles and parents' friends hugged me but when they spoke they broke open wounds that I had hidden.

It hurt to see my mother as a shrunken shell. We went shopping together for black clothes. I understood perfectly why my mother refused to wear any other color. I had just started wearing pastels the week before, and now I was back to black.

*   *   *

October 31, 1987

Dear Emily,

Halloween was our favorite time of year. I've always loved dressing up and playing someone else. My mother encouraged me, making elaborate costumes that she could turn into something else the next year. I remember the shiny, silky, gold dress that flowed to the ground. The first time I wore it I was the Statue of Liberty, with a flashlight torch and *The House at Pooh Corner* as my book. The next year I was an angel, with a halo and wings made from wire and crepe paper.

And I loved helping you with your costumes. Do you remember when we bought those curlers and bobby pins to make your red hair look like Annie's, from the musical? And the peacock outfit with the feathers stuck in a square of Styrofoam we painted? We strung it on a ribbon to tie on as a tail.

It was lonely the first time you wanted to go trick or treating with your friends. That Halloween you didn't want to go with Elizabeth, the baby. I took her, dressed as a pumpkin, on our block, for the neighbors to "ooh" and "aah." You wanted to be with Mandy. The two of you were ghosts. I guess that was the beginning of your struggle for independence.

Last year you announced you were too old for tick or treating, and refused to get a costume when Nick, Eric, and Elizabeth chose theirs. At the last minute Mandy asked you to go with her, so we dressed you up as an old man.

I'm not celebrating Halloween this year. I wasn't going to have a party anyway. I didn't feel like a party. I still miss you too much to plan fun.

But now Grandpa has died. This time of year won't be the same. He was the essence of comedy. His store of jokes was unending. They usually started with "A man went into a bar . . . ." His humor belied his worrying and serious soul. He was so grounded in reality but idealistic and creative. He so admired the particular trait of my mother that she passed down to me and me to you: no project was impossible. Just get thinking and doing, and something awe inspiring would emerge.

I'm so glad you got to know my father. Besides being a genius, he was wise. Who will give me sage advice now?

My father stood up for his beliefs, no matter what. I remember how proud I was when he was arrested in Englewood, sitting in for desegregation.

I valued my independence and refused to rely on my father. But now I so miss those Lake Tahoe blue eyes and the arms that could shield me from the world.

It's hard to believe that he's dead, too. Although he suffered with the cancer, I wasn't ready. Nor was my mother. At least you didn't have to face his death.

Love,
Mommy

CHAPTER 16

There's a certain slant of light,
Of Winter Afternoons—
That oppresses, like the Heft
Of cathedral tunes.

Heavenly Hurt it gives us;
We can find no scar;
But internal difference
Where the Meanings, are.

-Emily Dickinson

It was a sunny day in mid November, the seventy-five degree kind of day that reminds people why they moved to Phoenix. I turned into my driveway and stopped the car. It would be so easy to floor the accelerator and end my life. The car would crash into the garage wall, then the concrete block fence. No one else would be hurt. I wanted to be with Emily and Elizabeth, even if that meant death. I sat there for an eternity of five minutes, until my mother's face came to me. Not today, I sighed as I slowly drove the car into the garage.

I was alone and would be for hours. Dan was golfing then playing cards. The boys were with Diana until eight that night.

I went through the house, into the bedroom, and got into my well-worn, soft, purple flowered flannel nightgown. My head hurt and my body ached. The quilt scratched my legs. I was probably getting the flu that was going through the school. I took two extra strength Tylenols and hunkered down under the sheet and quilts with the television remote control. After trying all the channels, I gave up and turned on the radio I floated in and out of consciousness to the tunes of the Temptations, the Eagles, and others provided by the Golden Oldies station. Nick Simon's "American Tune" called out to me.

"And I don't know a soul who's not been battered,
I don't know a friend who feels at ease.
I don't know a dream that's not been shattered
Or driven to its knees."

I was sick but I was also falling down a deep well of depression. Maybe this would be the Big One that would black out everything. I put on the front porch light for Dan and the boys and went back to bed.

Life went on around me for the next few days, but I was not a willing participant. I called the substitute tape and took three sick days. After a day and half I was physically better, but I didn't want to get dressed and go out. I talked to no one except for basic needs, hiding under the cover of the flu. The air was too thick to breathe, weighing on my body, and gluing me to the bed.

On the third day I looked inside instead of allowing all the vague bad feelings to wall me in, brick by brick. It suddenly hit me that I could remain in limbo forever. I hated the way I felt, condemned to a purgatory of loss for an indefinite stay. I would have to make a decision to go on with my life without my daughters or to end my own life.

I was on the ceiling, looking down at my body, trying to decide what to do. I loved Dan, Nick, and Eric. How could I hurt them by killing myself? I couldn't put my mother, sister, and brother through another funeral so soon.

I was in a vise, holding me still while one end of me pulled toward suicide and my family pulled toward life. My fingers tried to undo the device, but they were clumsy and useless. I could escape into madness, but that would cause the same pain to others as suicide. Besides, I'd seen the movie of "One Flew Over the Cuckoo's Nest."

I dug way down inside myself, down into my stubbornness. I discovered a pocket of spiritualism, positive energy churning in my chest, growing little by little. I couldn't name it or grab ahold of it. It smelled like cinnamon, like my mother's pies cooling on the windowsill. I heard myself whispering, "I'll have another life, not the same one. A new life, with different joys and sorrows. Focus only on the present and the future."

I knew myself well enough to think in specific terms. I got up, took a shower, dressed, and went to my counseling appointment.

I fidgeted in the waiting room. This was my fourth weekly session with Roz. There were no big revelations yet, but it was a place where I cried.

Roz opened her door and welcomed me inside her office. She was an imposing figure. She had dark short hair that fell just right. Her clothes were stylish and expensive. She seemed just the right weight for her five foot seven inch perfectly proportioned body.

"How did it go this week?" Roz asked, as she had the other times.

I looked down and said softly, "I seriously considered killing myself."

"What made you decide not to do it?"

"I didn't want to hurt my family. It seemed the easy way out, though."

"What do you mean by 'the easy way out?'"

"I wouldn't have to deal with Emily's and Elizabeth's deaths. And I would be with them or not, depending on what comes after life. My dad's death is an overlay. I don't feel the same despair."

"The death of a parent is very sad, but if we've become mature adults, we can accept it. It is part of the cycle of life. The death of a child seems at odds with the life cycle. We all assume our children will outlive us. Next time you start getting depressed, you should call me right away."

"I didn't even think of that. I didn't even think about taking a Xanax. I didn't call my friends. I didn't talk to my husband. I isolated myself completely."

"Why didn't you feel able to talk to your husband?"

"I've already leaned on him so much. He's getting tired of being there for me all the time. I think he wants me to be better already."

"Has he said that to you?"

"Not in so many words."

"You should talk to him about how he's feeling."

"Maybe."

"Why didn't you feel able to talk with your friends?"

"Everyone worries about me, taking my emotional temperature. I'm in a glass cage. I don't want everyone talking and tsk-tsking. I want to be private. I can't relate to them like I used to. They were close to my daughters, so they're hurting too."

"How did you get out of your depression?"

"I willed myself out because I was scared I would stay in limbo forever. I've already heard stories about parents who visit their children's graves every day and I didn't want to be like that. I decided to try to go on with life. I'm going to prepare my resume to apply for principal and assistant principal jobs this spring. I'll get information from adoption attorneys. Do you think it's too soon? I'm going to be forty in March and I'm afraid I'm too old."

"I think it's the right thing for you. There aren't time rules that apply to everyone in the same way. I suggest that you try to write one of your friends a letter this week if you can't talk about these things on the telephone."

"I'll think about it."

"And call me if you feel yourself sliding into a depression."

"Okay, thanks. I'll see you next week."

* * *

November 23, 1987

Dear Emily,

Dan has bought a boat. It sits on a trailer in our garage, banishing the cars to the elements. It has a cabin underneath with a sleeping compartment. Nick and Eric can sleep on the bench seats in sleeping bags.

I'm reluctant to go out on the boat. It's something new, something that I never shared with you and Elizabeth. Part of me doesn't want to do anything you didn't share with me.

It's so quiet and beautiful at Canyon Lake. The steep walls reflect in the glass of the morning lake. We saw a bighorn sheep on top of the canyon yesterday. I wanted you and Wizzie to see it.

As the holidays loom before me, I'm remembering when you were just six months old. I wanted so badly to go to see my parents for Thanksgiving. I spent the fall making crafts to participate in a friend's boutique sale. I made cross stitch kits, some with feminist sayings like "Peace on earth, goodwill toward people," and "A woman's place is in the house . . . and the senate." I made hooked rugs that were advent calendars, appliqued bibs, and crocheted vests. I sold enough to buy our plane tickets and used all the unsold items as our holiday gifts for friends and relatives. You looked so cute in the brown velvet jumper I made, with the white satin turkey appliqued on the front. I miss you so much it's hard to bear.

Love,

Mommy

CHAPTER 17

There is another sky,
Ever serene and fair,
And there is another sunshine
Though it be darkness there

-Emily Dickinson

"Dan, I've been thinking about babies," I said as I snuggled next to him. The warmth from his body spread to my arms and chest, warding off some of the chill I always felt these days.

"What about them?"

"When I sent for information about adoptions, I got a letter from an attorney who specializes in surrogate parenting. He's in a firm that also does private adoptions. These days the eggs of a woman and the semen from a man can be mixed together in a dish to get fertilized eggs. The eggs are then put back in the womb."

"Are we talking about us? I thought you didn't have the equipment any more."

"I don't have a uterus but I probably have the eggs in my ovaries. In our case we would need another woman's body to implant the egg. It's called surrogate motherhood."

"Are you serious about this?"

"I talked to Susan and she offered to be the surrogate mother."

"I don't know about that. I think it would be better if it was a stranger. If Susan did it, it would make all the relationships screwy."

"Then you'd consider doing it?"

Dan gave out a deep sigh. "I guess . . . . if that's what you want."

"Let's go to Los Angeles and talk to the lawyer."

"Figures he's in L.A."

"You are the most wonderful, understanding man in the world."

"I know," Dan said as he nuzzled the top of my hair.

*   *   *

It was early March when Dan parked the rental car in the underground parking provided by the posh office building in Beverly Hills. The suite was on the tenth floor. The reception area of the law offices exuded luxury. The magazines on the coffee tables were all the latest issues. The receptionist was a beautiful and fashionably attired young woman. After a short wait we were ushered into a conference room with a huge black smoked glass table and deep comfortable black leather chairs.

A portly man in a gray suit that was a size too small said, "Hi, I'm Ronald Taft. Please call me Ron. I understand you're interested in obtaining a surrogate mother."

"We're interested in getting information about the process," Dan said.

"It's quite simple, really. We work with a team of doctors. I've set up an appointment for an examination for you today, Annie, to make sure you're in good general health. You'll set the date for a laparoscopy to see if your ovaries have the eggs. Dan gives them semen, some of which they test. The rest of his semen is frozen until the eggs are harvested. Annie goes on some drugs to get more than one egg when she ovulates. When the time is right, you come here and our doctors harvest the eggs with another laparoscopy. The eggs are fertilized by Dan's sperm in a dish. At least two eggs are implanted in the uterus of the surrogate mother. If an egg starts to grow, we're on. There's no guarantee that the fertilized eggs will take hold, but we've had sixty-four births in six years. It's very exciting."

"What is the possibility of success with each try?" Dan asked.

"About ten to twenty percent," Ron replied.

"Have you had any problems with the surrogates wanting to keep the babies?"

"No, we haven't. We have a very careful screening process in place. Our psychologist gives the prospective surrogates a battery of tests as well as the ones the medical doctors do."

"My best friend wants to be the surrogate mother," I said.

"I don't recommend that. We won't get involved if the couple knows the surrogate mother. There's too much opportunity for heartache."

"That's just what I thought," Dan said.

Dan asked more questions, but my mind was trying to picture a baby with my own and Dan's genes. It would be one tall kid.

Ron gave Dan the name and address of the clinic as well as directions on how to get there. The nurses and doctors at the clinic were polite, but I didn't get any warm feelings. The doctor declared me healthy and set the laparoscopy for April.

When we were back on the plane, Dan asked, "Are you still interested in doing this?"

"Definitely."

"Okey dokey," Dan said. Then he whispered in my ear, "You know how much I love you if I'm willing to jerk off in a bottle."

I threw my head back and laughed.

"I appreciate it. I wonder if they'll let me help you," I said as I surreptitiously grabbed him.

*   *   *

Susan and I hugged each other in the midst of the baggage claim area of Phoenix's Sky Harbor Airport. It was late March and Susan had flown in for a ladies' weekend to mark our fortieth birthdays. Nick and Eric were with their mom and Dan was at a golf tournament in Lake Havasu.

We caught each other up on gossip on the ride back to my house.

"What does the tour master have planned?" asked Susan.

"I thought we'd visit Desert Botanical Gardens tomorrow. On the way back there are some shops too cute to pass by. Tomorrow night we have reservations at an excellent restaurant. On Sunday I thought we'd go for a ride in the desert. How does that sound?"

"It works for me."

"I brought someone with me for dinner tonight," Susan said as she opened a hatbox. She took out the biggest lobster I'd ever seen. She whipped up a lobster dinner and we stuffed ourselves on lobster, pasta, and sourdough bread. After we cleaned the kitchen, I put a fire in the fireplace, even though it wasn't cold.

Susan uncorked some wine as we pulled the love seats to face the fire.

"This weekend feels like the times when your parents would go away and ask me to stay with you, Susan. Remember when we drank the whole bottle of gin mixed with grape juice while we watched the Miss America pageant?"

"Yeah, and we went down to China Wall to get egg rolls," Susan added.

"On the way back you dropped the house key. We got down on our hands and knees looking for it, laughing so hard we rolled in a pile of leaves and twigs and peed in our pants."

"And my parents never suspected anything because they thought you were the model teenager."

"Ah yes, the wanton ways of our past. Now we are the middle aged matrons we never thought we'd be," I said.

"I may be middle aged but I am definitely not a matron,"

Susan said, taking out a joint. "But where, oh where is the passion of our youth?"

"How long has it been since just you and David had a little vacation?" I asked.

Susan paused to consider that. "I don't think we've had one since Vanessa was born."

"Vanessa is four years old! I suggest you start with some weekends away. Sex is a whole 'nother scene when you're away from home without kids."

"Maybe I'll arrange a getaway. The Saran wrap didn't work."

"You didn't!"

"Yeah, I did. Vanessa was at a friend's house. I got naked and packaged my body in plastic. But it was a hot day and David had a late emergency meeting at work. I got so sweaty I finally peeled it off myself and jumped in the pool. By the time David got home, I was back in my shorts and tee shirt."

"You are too much! My sex life is the least of my worries. I'm going to have a lot of money soon," I said. "I like to spend money as much as the next person, but I feel guilty that I'll never have to worry about money again because Emily and Elizabeth died."

"My opinion is that someone owes you big time for your pain and suffering," Susan said. "That's a debt that can never be paid off."

"We'll use some to adopt a baby or pay for a surrogate mother," I said. "We need to move into another house, mine has too many bittersweet memories. Dan wants to start a roofing company with his boss. I'm a little leery because I think he's a slime bucket. And I'll probably go shopping when I feel blue. It helps."

"I don't know how you stand it," Susan said.

"The secret is that I don't. The only way for me to survive is to repress the pain. I try not to think about my first life too much. The one I had with Elizabeth and Emily and Rob is gone, and I can't do anything to get it back. That life got sucked into the Black Hole of Yesterdays. It doesn't take a PhD to figure out that if I dwell on what I lost, the living part of my family feels like they're unimportant. I'm concentrating on a life with Dan, Eric, Nick, and maybe a baby."

"You're truly amazing, Annie," Susan said. "Tell me more about this surrogate mother thing,"

"We met with the lawyer. He nixed the idea of you being the surrogate"

"I'm disappointed. I loved being pregnant. Do you think it was because you wouldn't have to pay me?"

"I don't know, but Dan didn't think it was a good idea either. I want another child, no doubt about that. I don't know how long we'd have to wait for an adoptive baby or if we can get one. I'm forty, we're different religions, and Dan has two sons. I don't think we'd be a priority couple."

"Couldn't you specify the gender in an adoption?"

"The more things you specify, the longer the wait. If I could have a baby myself, I would get pregnant right away, and I'd gladly take a girl or a boy. In my heart of hearts I probably long for a girl, but I'm not sure that's the best for the child. Everyone would compare a baby girl to Elizabeth and Emily. They have angel status and no opportunity to ruin that. That's not healthy.

"A baby has a right not to live in someone else's shadow. Dan would like an older child, but there aren't many American orphans, and I don't have the kind of job where I could spend a few months in another country. Someone I know works with foster parents, and she said that state agencies aren't truthful about the problems of older children. I think our family has had enough problems. So we're going for a baby."

"What are the chances of the surrogate mother arrangement happening?" Susan asked.

"The success rate for in vitro fertilization is relatively low. Once a surrogate is found, I have to take fertility drugs up the yazoo to increase the number of eggs I ovulate. Enough about that. Let's raid the cupboard." I said.

We had chocolate orgasms on See's candies.

Annie, Susan B., and Linda having high tea for Annie's fortieth birthday

*   *   *

Dr. Bethune was a short man with perfect teeth. I was lying on the operating table, looking at the doctor's gleaming white, straight teeth as he talked to me about the surgery he was about to perform. I tuned in and out of his monologue.

I was nervous but not afraid. I had a laparoscopy a few months after Elizabeth was born for a tubal ligation, recovered easily, and was up and around the same day.

I couldn't keep my eyes open. When I did open them, Dan was sitting beside my bed.

"How do you feel?' Dan asked.

"Groggy."

"While you were sleeping, I was bopping my baloney into a cup in a bathroom. Talk about feeling stupid! I haven't jacked myself off since I was fifteen."

"I appreciate it, Dan. I think I'll just sleep for a minute."

When I woke up the second time, a dull ache enveloped my body, punctuated by sharp pains. I knew from the other laparoscopy that the sharp pains were bubbles of gas that the doctor pumped in my stomach. The gas traveled everywhere after the surgery.

"Time to go back to Susan's," Dan said. We're lucky she lives so close to L.A. Do you need help getting dressed?"

"No, I can manage," I said as I struggled off the bed onto the cold tile floor.

I wrestled with my bra and finally let Dan help me.

I leaned on him as we walked to the car. The ride to the Susan's, in Manhattan Beach, seemed to take forever. When we finally got there Dan helped me out. I lurched forward as a sharp pain pierced my right shoulder. Susan and David clucked over me but I went straight to the bed. Dan took my shoes off.

"Do you want anything to eat or drink?" Susan asked.

"I'd like some water and a new body. This surgery was a snap when I had it before. I hope I feel a lot better tomorrow."

Dr. Bethune called that evening to tell me that my ovaries had started to atrophy and were not currently ovulating, but would probably work with medication. When I asked about the side effects of the medication, he mentioned severe mood swings.

Mood swings. I was finally feeling less depressed and a little more connected to my family. Was I mentally strong enough to withstand the side effects of the medication or would they tip me back into another deep depression?

I stayed in bed most of the weekend, venturing out to the dining room for Susan's gourmet meals. I was surprised at how badly I felt. I would have to go through this every other month to harvest eggs. I dismissed my doubts about whether I could physically withstand what it took to use a surrogate mother by concentrating on how wonderful a baby would be.

Before we went back to Phoenix, we signed a contract with Ronald Taft and gave him a check for $10,000. Dan had arranged for a ninety day loan through a banker friend.

"How long is the waiting period for an in vitro fertilization surrogate?" I asked.

"It's about three to four months," Ron said.

"With only a ten percent chance of success," I said, "we're also going to register with an independent adoption attorney."

"I think that's a good idea. My partner Durand Cook has an excellent program."

"We have his materials. If a surrogate is not found for a long time, or Dan and my results are not positive, or if one of us dies before a surrogate is signed, is the agreement void?" I asked.

"We spend $2000 up front to advertise, so that part of the retainer is not refundable," Ron said.

"I want to make it clear that we are only interested in the in vitro fertilization, not artificial insemination using the surrogate's egg," I said.

"I understand," Ron said and he stood up to signal the end of the meeting. "I'm confident that we will be able to accommodate you."

"Thank you," Dan said as they shook hands.

*   *   *

May 1, 1988

Dear Emily,

Mother's Day is a storm that's forecast for next week. Am I still a mother if you're dead? Being your mother meant the most to me. Mother's Guilt is intruding. I should write equal letters to Elizabeth. But you are old enough to understand. I am crazy! I'm asking a dead child to understand me!

Dan and I are trying to have a baby. A child would never replace you or Elizabeth. There will never be anyone as wonderful or anyone I'll be as close with. Maybe we were too close.

You know I had a hysterectomy, but these days doctors can take my eggs and his sperm outside our bodies, mix them, then implant them in someone else who will give us the baby after it's born. Writing it out like that makes me realize how weird the process is!

I asked Mandy's mom about adoption. She's on a government adoption board. She said there are very few "orphans" these days. Most children who are up for adoption have been abused. I don't know if I have enough inner strength to deal with such a child. She didn't recommend it because the agencies aren't truthful about all the kid's problems.

Nick and Eric are doing great. Nick plays the trumpet and is going to Camp Pacific with Mr. Plummer. Both boys started Little League. Nick made it to the Majors! I know Eric misses Elizabeth but he won't talk about it. They're going to spend Mother's Day with their mother, then come home for a late dinner with us. I hate sharing them!

You and Elizabeth will always be the lights of my life.

Love,
Mommy

CHAPTER 18

Time does go on—

I tell it gay to those who suffer now—they shall survive—

There is a sun—they don't believe it now—

-Emily Dickinson

Dan said he had planned something special for Mother's Day, and to have my bag packed with casual clothes and one nice dress by Saturday afternoon.

I had already taken a Valium when Dan got home from golfing late Saturday afternoon. He took a quick shower, threw his things into his bag, and loaded up the car. We explored the Arcadia section of town while I jotted down the addresses of some houses for sale.

We drove onto the back side of Camelback Mountain to John Gardiner's Tennis Ranch. I had never been there before so it held no booby trap memories. What a thoughtful husband I had.

We went to our casita, unpacked our bags, and hung up clothing.

"How about a roll in the hay?" Dan asked.

"Okay with me."

Dan walked over and gave me a hug. He started to stroke my hair, then my back. He slowly and carefully took off my clothes, then his own. We lay on the bed. He got little response from me. We made love. I took comfort in the closeness of his body.

As we lay entwined afterward, I confided my doubts about using a surrogate mother.

"I don't know if I want to take the strong medications I'll need to get eggs ready. I'm just starting to feel human again. I'll never feel like my old self again, but I'm starting to be a new person. Some happiness seeps in. The fertility medications may cause big mood swings. One day I'll be happy, higher than a kite. The next day I'll be low as a ditch."

"That sounds like a lot of fun," Dan said.

"It took me five days to bounce back after the laparoscopy. I'd have to go to California every other month and do it. I've been applying for administrative positions. I don't think the principal or assistant principal can be absent so much."

"Mmm," Dan said noncommittally.

"How important is it for you that a baby have our genes?" I asked.

"Annie, I'll do whatever you want. Don't do this for me. I have no problem loving an adopted child. Once we get a kid, it's ours."

"I've been feeling desperate, probably anticipating Mother's Day and not realizing it. This surrogate mother thing is nuts, isn't it?"

Dan let out a sigh. "I was hoping you'd see it that way sooner or later."

"Do you feel adoption is just as crazy?"

"No, that's normal as far as I'm concerned."

Okay, I'll look at the paperwork from the adoption attorneys."

We dressed for dinner. Dan looked me over from head to toe and said, "You clean up good."

"You look pretty spiffy yourself," I replied as I got on tiptoe to kiss him on the cheek.

We went up to the main lodge and ate in the glass-walled dining room that displayed a twilight view of the mountains and the twinkling lights of the houses.

We walked hand in hand back to our casita in the cool night air.

"You can see more stars here," I said, "even though it's only ten miles from our house."

"The downtown lights are on the other side of Camelback Mountain, so they don't obliterate the night sky."

We took off our clothes and got into bed. Dan watched a ball game on television while I read a Sue Grafton murder mystery. I could feel my agitation start so I got up and took a Valium. Dan slept with his arms around me.

Early the next morning I felt like my brain was wrapped in cotton but I couldn't fall back to sleep.

"Dan," I whispered.

"Huh?"

"I need to talk about Emily and Elizabeth. I don't want to act like they never existed on Mother's Day."

"Okay, I'm listening," he said as he put another pillow under his head.

"Will you tell me something about them? Just a memory you have of them."

"Okay. I remember how much Elizabeth liked it when I would tease her. When I tried to grab her belly button she would let out a scream that could dry up a cow's milk."

I smiled but tears stung behind my eyes.

"Elizabeth was the most beautiful baby I'd ever seen," I said. "She was small and perfect. She hardly ever cried. I figured she was going to be a docile child. Was I ever wrong! She was so stubborn and independent!"

"Now Emily was harder to get to know," Dan said. "At first I thought she was stuck up and I didn't measure up to her idea of a suitable stepfather. When we went on that vacation to the White Mountains to fish, she and I got a chance to talk. She confided that she wanted to be an actress. She was crazy about that acting camp she went to. Although the odds of making it were slim, I encouraged her to go for it. We were closer after that."

"I didn't know she wanted to go into theater! I thought it was just fun for her to be involved, like a hobby. Emily could be a rascal, too. One day she came home, she was about eleven, with a terror stricken look on her face. She finally got the courage to tell me that she had thrown out her retainer with her lunch tray. I called the dentist and found out it would be three hundred dollars for another one. I didn't have the money, so we changed into grubby clothes and charged up to the school, to the cafeteria dumpster. Emily got into the dumpster to pick through the garbage while I stood on the side, sifting through the higher stuff. She finally found it, wrapped up in a napkin. She popped it right back into her mouth! I had a fit and made her take it home and soak it in mouthwash to kill the germs."

I buried my head in Dan's shoulder and let the tears flow. He put his arms around me and held me gently until the crying stopped.

"I'm starved!" said Dan. "Let's get ready and eat breakfast, then we'll go look at some of the houses in Arcadia."

I put on shorts for the first time of the season. They were new and I checked them out from all angles in the mirror to see if I looked decent in them. I was satisfied that I wouldn't be embarrassed by my appearance.

We left after breakfast and looked at several houses in Arcadia. One was a fix-up that Dan liked but I had reservations about how much time and money it would take to get it in shape. We saw a yellow one that had just been remodeled. It was out of our price range, but I starred the address.

The last one we looked at was a huge, modern, two story house on a cul de sac. It was all white, including white ceramic tiles on the floors, and empty. Dan loved its enormity. I recoiled from its sterility until we entered the living room. One wall of the room was a trapezoidal window that looked out on Camelback Mountain. The mountain moved me. I couldn't say why, but it was my mountain.

"Isn't it just breathtaking?" the realtor of the Open House chimed in, breaking the spell.

When we got back in the car, Dan and I looked into each other's faces.

"But it's so white!" I said. "It's a Great White Wonder."

"We can paint a couple of rooms," Dan said. "Besides, I know you can make any house a home. That's the one I want. What about you?"

"I'd buy it just for the view from the living room," I said. "But they're asking so much!"

"Yeah, I'll find out how much room for bargaining there is. Time to go to the golf course."

Dan was being sweet by playing golf with me. He was a scratch player and I didn't even have a handicap yet. When I did, it would be the highest there was. I hit my first tee shot out of bounds. He just smiled indulgently.

*   *   *

The next evening I wrote Ron of our decision to cancel the contract for the surrogate mother, asking him to transfer our deposit to his partner. I filled out the application forms for two adoption attorneys in California. One of them was the law partner of Ron, and another was in northern California. My cousin, who's an attorney and had adopted a baby, had given me a referral list for Arizona and California. The brochure for the major private adoption center in Arizona turned me off. The fee to get on a waiting list was very high, about $15,000. Once accepted, a nonrefundable donation of $10,000 was made to the center's nonprofit arm to pay for the upkeep of birth mothers, but this was a blind contribution with no accounting. That's how they got around the Arizona law that adoptive families couldn't pay for the living expenses of the birth mother.

The California attorneys wanted a $10,000 payment, but this was for an account for a particular birth mother and attorney fees. The adoptive parents were advised of all payments for the living expenses of the birth mother. This sounded more kosher to me.

I also contacted the county court system for the papers to start the proceedings to certify us as an adoptive family in Arizona. A chink of sunlight shone in my life.

*   *   *

I sat in the reception area of a lawyer I'd never met, flipping through the pages of a month-old *Newsweek* without reading a word. I put the magazine down and took out a thick envelope from my purse. I read over for the tenth time the settlement that the insurance company for the airlines had sent. It looked fine to me, but I wanted to be sure.

A very thin, short, bald man came out to greet me.

"I'm Amil Ajamie," he said as he extended his hand.

I shook his hand and introduced myself. He led me into his office. There were files stacked on the desk and the floor.

"I was told your area of expertise is contracts," I said. "I want to pay you by the hour to look over a wrongful death settlement and check out the details of the papers they want me to sign. I've already had an attorney in California, who's an accountant and an expert in structured settlements, check the offer."

"What were the particulars of the situation?"

I cleared my throat and stretched my lips over my teeth. "Both of my daughters were killed in the plane crash last August outside Detroit."

"Please accept my sympathies for your loss. Such a tragedy. How did this settlement offer come about?"

"My husband and I met with the representative from the insurance company. They sent me several offers, but this is the one I think is the best. They can never give me back what I lost. I can't have any more children, but we're applying to adopt a child. We can't afford to pay the fees on our salaries."

"I'd like some time to look this over."

"Sure. But I want to get this over with as soon as possible. I need the money to move to another house. It's hard to live in a place with the ghosts of my daughters." My voice cracked just before the end of the sentence. My throat constricted in pain and tears stung behind my eyes.

"It shouldn't take more than a day or two. Let me have your phone number and I'll call you."

As he was escorting me out, I turned to him and said, "If everything's in order, I want you to call the attorney who wrote the offer and tell him that I accept it."

"Certainly. I'll let you know as soon as possible."

My shoulders relaxed to a slump as I rode the elevator down to my car. There were so many things going on I was glad to give someone else the responsibility for the settlement. Dan and I were working with a real estate agent and looking at houses. We are still considering the Great White Wonder we had seen on Mother's Day. The paperwork for the county certification adoption was time consuming. There was less than a month of school left and so much to do. Sometimes I just wanted to climb up a tree and stay there, observing the world without having to participate.

*   *   *

Two weeks later Dan and I sat in Amil Ajamie's office. I looked at the check he had put into my shaking hands.

"They really are dead," I said as tears overflowed, burning my eyes.

Dan leaned over from his chair and put his hand on my arm.

"Thank you for your help, Mr. Ajamie," Dan said. "It's been tough going for Annie, but she's an incredible woman. I don't think there are many people who could go one with life as she has. You'll never meet anyone as strong as her. I don't think I would have done half as well."

"You certainly saved a lot of money, time, and emotional distress by doing the legwork on this yourselves," the attorney said.

It seemed natural to have them talking about me as if I wasn't there. I was on the sidelines, observing the scene, trying desperately not to feel anything.

Dan and the attorney talked a short time.

"Annie, it's time to go," Dan said as put his hand on my back.

"Are you okay?" Dan asked when we got back home.

"No, I'll never be okay, but I'm as good as I'm going to get."

"Do you want to make an offer on the Great White Wonder?"

"Arcadia has trees and grass like this home. I would like to be able to see Camelback Mountain every day," I said. "Isn't it too expensive for us?"

"They've reduced the price to within our range."

"Will you talk to the real estate agency and just take care of the whole thing?"

"Sure, I'd be glad to do that. At least it's something I can do for you."

*   *   *

May 15, 1988

Dear Emily,

Today I went to a lawyer's office and received a check from the airlines, a settlement. The worst part is that it means you are really dead. There's a finality and closure with legal arrangements. I came home, stripped off my clothes and flung them on the bed. I turned on the shower and waited until it got hot. Then I stepped into the steady, hard stream of water and let it cascade over me, drowning out my sobs and camouflaging my tears. I feel so guilty taking the money. I shouldn't profit from your deaths. But what if I really go crazy and can't work? I'll give some of the money to the Temple, some to charity. I know you'd approve of that. You're sponsoring a child for the Camp Pacific trip. There will be an Emily Geiger Award at Clarendon, with a scholarship for high school expenses. The yearbook is dedicated to you this year. They're using a picture from the wedding. You look so beautiful. And Elizabeth is sponsoring a child for summer camp at the Temple.

We're buying a new house. I'll miss your ghosts, but it's hard to go on with my life when I see you in every nook of our house.

I'll love you forever and a day.

Love,
Mommy

CHAPTER 19

Hope is a strange invention—
A Patent of the Heart—
In unremitting action
Yet never wearing out—

                    -Emily Dickinson

"This could be our big break!" said Elissa, a friend from administration classes at ASU. It was late May and we were on our way into a conference sponsored by AWARE, an organization formed to set up an "old girls' network" to help women get into school administration.

"I was reading the *Arizona School Administrator* last night," Elissa said, "and there were quite a few positions available. I've heard that a lot of women get jobs because this conference shows us how to do the paperwork right and we get to practice interviewing."

"I think I'm ready for a new challenge," I said. "There have been so many changes in my life I might as well go for one more."

After we registered, we went to separate workshops. When I walked into the session on resume writing, I recognized the presenter as the budget director I had seen more than a year ago at a school board meeting about decisions that affected Emily's gifted program.

"Hi, I'm Annie Weissman. I recognized you from school board meetings."

"Yes, I remember you. I'm no longer with that district. I'm now an assistant superintendent for Sunnyback Elementary School District."

"Congratulations!"

"Thanks. Didn't you send in a resume to be critiqued?"

"Yes I did."

She looked over my appearance while she was sifting through papers until she found my resume. I felt good in the blue pinstripe suit my mother had made.

"We have a little time before the session starts, let me give you some pointers."

I was amazed at how a format change, some editing, and adding improved my resume.

"There's an opening for an assistant principal in my district. The closing date is Wednesday. I strongly encourage you to apply."

"Thanks, I'll get the application on Monday."

"Wear pumps with small heels to the interview."

I looked down at my blue sandal heels. Did shoes really make a difference? I decided to visit the large sized shoe store over the weekend.

The resume session was very informative about cover letters and the accompanying paperwork for applications.

We checked the job board before we left, jotting down the information for openings.

"I'm jazzed," I said on the way home. "I'm ready for a new life."

"I'm tired of the paperwork in the classroom."

"I think there's even more paperwork when you get into administration. I'm ready to have the power to set the tone of the school, and help people make changes."

"Are you applying for the assistant principal job in Sunnyback?" Elissa asked.

"Sure am!"

"Me, too. I hope one of us gets it."

Elissa and I said our good byes and good lucks.

The house was empty. Dan and the boys were still out at the golf course. I took the time to go through my desk drawers and find all the necessary transcripts and certificates to attach to an administrative application. I made the suggested changes to my resume and took it up to the copy store so it could be typed into a computer. I picked beige paper for the resume, as had been suggested, and bought some extra sheets for a cover letter. I typed up several drafts before I was satisfied. My packet looked much more professional than anything I had ever written.

This might be my lucky break.

*   *   *

I waited nervously in the small lobby of Sunnyback Elementary District Office. I scanned the notes I had in the manila folder on my lap. I glanced down and nodded at my new navy blue pumps. They had even been on sale.

I was ushered into the boardroom where I faced the interview team made up of the superintendent, the principal of the school, a parent, a teacher, and the assistant superintendent who had presented the resume session at the AWARE conference.

The team sat in the board members' high back comfortable chairs. I sat down at the end of a long rectangular table in a folding chair, feeling like a suspect at an interrogation.

The questions the interview team asked were ones I had anticipated. I paused to collect my thoughts, and glance at my notes, before answering each one. When the superintendent asked if I had any questions, I asked each member of the team a direct question that required at least a few sentences to answer. When I asked the principal what qualities she wanted in an assistant principal, I caught the smile and the enthusiasm that accompanied the woman's words.

I skipped to my car in the parking lot, and yelled "Hot damn!" after I got in.

*   *   *

A week later my principal sent the secretary down to cover my class.

It's probably Sara's mother, I thought, ready to chew me out for suggesting that her child ruined a library book.

The principal motioned me into his empty office.

"Sunnyback District just called. They wanted to know how I thought you'd do as an assistant principal. I told them how knowledgeable you are. Somehow they had heard about your daughters' deaths and wanted to know if you were emotionally stable. I assured them you handled the situation well and that your work hadn't suffered."

"I really appreciate your recommendation," I said.

"I think you have the job, Annie!"

"What?"

"Don't say anything to anyone because I probably wasn't supposed to tell you. We'll call you to the office when they call."

"I'll act surprised, I promise."

I left the office and leaped into the air and shouted "Hallelujah!" Then I skipped all the way back to the library.

The call came an hour later. The director of personnel told me that he would present a recommendation to hire me at the next Board meeting.

I called Dan's office and left a message with the news. Later Dan came home with flowers and took Nick, Eric, and me to dinner to celebrate my entrance into administration.

*   *   *

The next week Dan and I got on another airplane and headed for Los Angeles to meet an adoption attorney.

I had to take a Valium to get myself on the plane. We drove to Beverly Hills and went into the same building and up to the same offices where we had seen Ron, the lawyer for surrogate mothers. This time we were seeing Durand Cook, Ron's partner, who specialized in adoptions. The same pretty secretary led us to the same conference room, but this time I was more observant, more my old self. I admired the view from the smoke colored windows.

Durand Cook was a tall good-looking man who had jet black hair. He wore a well-tailored gray suit. After the introductions, he got down to business.

"Tell me why you want to adopt," he asked.

"My daughters were killed in the plane crash outside Detroit last August. I had a hysterectomy so I can't have any more children. I can never replace my daughters, but I have room in my heart for more children."

"My sons are eight and eleven, and live with us," Dan said. "We just feel we have more parenting we want to do."

"I read over your application, so I knew about your daughters, Annie. I'm sorry for your loss."

"Thank you."

"Let me tell you about the process. We run classified ads in newspapers around the country, looking for pregnant women who choose not to keep their babies. They come out here and we send them to a doctor for a physical. Our psychologist talks with them. Then I talk with them and show them a video about private adoption. Not all the girls and women choose to go forward with the process. If they do decide to go with our program, we get them a place to live and money for food. Now some of the birth mothers live with their parents, so the expenses are less. We introduce the birth mother to an adoptive family, with me orchestrating the meeting. Then I conference separately with the birth mother and the adoptive parents to see if it's a match. There is a waiting period. In each state it's different. In California it's six months before the birth mother can sign the final papers to give up the baby."

"How long is the wait to meet a birth mother?"

"If you want to proceed, it will be between three to nine months, depending on how many stipulations you want."

"What do you mean 'stipulations'?" asked Dan.

"Stipulations are eye color, height, weight, musical ability, intelligence, etc. of the birth parents or sex of the child. I'm looking at your application and you made no stipulations except race."

"And I want a birth mother who isn't going to change her mind," I said. "I don't think I could take a loss like that. Arizona does not look kindly on interracial adoptions, that's why we want a white baby. We don't want any legal problems."

"You'll need to hire an attorney in Phoenix to take care of the Arizona part of the adoption. Do you have any other questions?"

"Does the birth mother have any contact with the adoptive parents after the baby is born?" I asked.

"Not unless the adoptive family requests it. Sometimes the birth mothers want an annual letter with a picture. That's up to the adoptive parents, and it is routed through our office. I'll leave you alone to discuss it. Let my secretary know when you've come to a decision."

Dan looked at me and lifted his eyebrows. I nodded.

"We don't need any time to discuss it. We like the way you operate," Dan said. "I believe you already have a deposit from your partner."

"Yes, I'll need a check for an additional six thousand dollars."

I took out my checkbook, wrote the check, and handed it to Durand Cook.

"There is a financial risk," he said. "Just because you pay for the living expenses of the mother does not entitle you to her child. She can change her mind at any time and you do not get your money back."

"We understand," Dan said.

"We'll call you when we find a birth mother for you," he said.

Dan and I drove to the airport and boarded a plane for northern California. We rented another car and drove to see the other adoption attorney that had been recommended by my cousin. The attorney's office was in a strip shopping center. It wasn't shabby, but it was only a cut above it, quite a contrast to the plush offices of Durand Cook.

The attorney was a trim, healthy looking fellow. He invited us into his cluttered office.

"Tell us about the process of adopting," Dan said.

"We advertise for birth mothers and advise you to advertise yourselves. Each adoptive family makes an album with pictures of themselves, their homes, and their pets, and a statement about why they want to adopt a child. Birth mothers look through the albums and choose an adoptive family. I then contact the adoptive family who pays for the living and medical expenses of the birth mother, with a careful accounting from this office."

"Do we meet the birth mother?"

"No, I act as the go-between."

"How long would it be before we got a baby?" I asked.

"That's hard to calculate, but the average wait is nine to fifteen months. The process starts as soon as you open a ten thousand dollar account with us and send your album. It's a gamble. If the birth mother backs out, you do not get a refund on the money you paid for her living expenses."

Dan and the attorney talked about some particulars and then sports, but my mind was elsewhere. I didn't like the vibes I got from this attorney.

Dan thanked him for his time and we left.

As soon as we got back in the rented car, Dan turned to me and said, "I don't think we need to bother with this guy. He's not in the big leagues like the one this morning."

"You're right. Let's put all our eggs in the Durand Cook basket."

*   *   *

The next evening Carol and I were in the steam room of her health club, relaxing. I sat up, with the towel wrapped around me while Carol lounged on her back on the bench, with her towel underneath her.

"You know it's probably almost as hot outside as it is in here," I said.

"I just love the heat! I'm so glad I moved to Phoenix," Carol said.

"I'm glad you did, too. I read somewhere that any time there is a major change in your life, it means added stress. My stress level should be off the scale: death, new kids, new house, and new job."

"You always look like you can handle it."

"I know, I find it almost impossible to ask for help or admit weakness. I'm lucky that Dan is there to shoulder his part and more without asking. He's really taken care of the whole deal with the house, including the moving company. He's arranged for the painting of some of the rooms before we move in." I rolled onto my back, covering myself with the small white towel.

"I'll plan a packing party next weekend."

"That's very sweet of you. I'm kind of afraid to pack because I know I'll find all kinds of mementos from Emily and Elizabeth." I bent down and mopped up the sweat and tears in and around my eyes with my towel.

"Consider it done."

"I leave for a week long 'Principals' Academy' up in Flagstaff the day after we move. Elissa and I signed up for it together."

"That's great! I love to see women breaking into school administration. Tell me about your trip to see the adoption attorneys yesterday."

I filled her in on the details.

"I thought the wait for babies was years."

"So did I," I said, "but he said since we put so few stipulations, it won't take very long."

"What do you mean?"

"We didn't ask for parents who were rocket scientists or any particular looks. We asked for a healthy white infant whose mother wouldn't change her mind."

"Are you certified for adoption yet?"

"No, I'm hoping that will happen before anything else does, but the molasses of the bureaucracy moves slowly. What's happening with you?"

"Zobi called me over the weekend. She has finally realized she has a problem and she no longer blames everything on me. AA has really helped her. It felt so good when she told me she was done blaming me, and she was taking the responsibility. She's going to take the GED test and go to a community college next fall."

"I'm so happy for you! How's Patrick?" I asked. He was the same age as Emily and it was hard to hear about what he was doing. Usually Carol waited until I asked before she discussed him.

"He's okay. He's going through adolescence and is starting to rebel. Poor Terry is taking the brunt of it. Maybe Patrick's figured out what a schmuck his father is. He never writes or calls him. It's pathetic."

"Poor Patrick, that's hard for any kid to understand or accept a father's rejection. I don't look forward to the teen age years."

"I do envy you a little, adopting a baby. Terry and I decided that we would do the baby thing vicariously, through you and Dan."

A woman entered the steam room and sat down on her towel.

"I'm about to faint," I said. "Let's get out of here, take a cold shower, and get a beer."

"You're on, girl!"

*   *   *

I saw the note on the message board in the hall of the Northern Arizona University building where I was headed for a seminar session. "Urgent! Call Dan at his office!"

Shit, what's wrong now? I thought. I found the nearest pay phone and had to clasp my hands behind me so I wouldn't strangle the man who was using the phone. He finally put the receiver back in its place.

I tapped my fingers as I waited for the secretary to forward the call to Dan.

"What's the emergency?" I asked as soon as Dan answered.

"We got a call this morning from Durand Cook's office. He wants us to fly over this weekend and meet a birth mother. I have to call him back this morning to let him know if we're coming."

"We saw him less than two weeks ago!"

"I understand, but he must have made us a priority. What do you want to do?"

"We aren't certified for adoption in Arizona yet!"

"He said the woman was four months along so we should have plenty of time for that," Dan said.

"What do you think?"

"Let's go for it!"

"My meetings are over tomorrow about four so I'll drive straight home so we can leave the next morning."

"That sounds fine, I'll make the plane reservations and let Diana know that the boys won't be over this weekend."

"I can't believe this is happening so fast!"

"Let's get it on."

"I love you and I'll see you tomorrow. I've missed you."

"Okey dokey. We'll go out to dinner when you get home."

I drove home in record time.

*   *   *

CHAPTER 20

Wonder—is not precisly Knowing
And not precisely Knowing not—
A beautiful but bleak condition
He has not lived who has not felt—

-Emily Dickinson

I was having a hard time concentrating on what Durand Cook was saying. I was nervous but excited to be meeting someone who might be carrying my next child.

We were in the conference room, getting prepared to meet a birth mother. At eight years old, Eric still didn't quite understand the circumstances, but Nick at almost eleven understood that the family was "looking over a mother for the new baby." I tuned back in as Durand was describing the birth mother, wondering at what point we had gotten on a first name basis.

"Tanya is living with her boyfriend, but he is not the baby's father. She's twenty-nine, and she's been on her own since she was sixteen. She hasn't been in contact with her family since then. She drove out here from the Midwest after she saw our ad in a local paper. Any questions before you meet her?"

"How do we know she hasn't taken drugs or been drunk while she's been pregnant?" I asked.

"She signed a release form that allows me to see the results of her medical tests. She got a checkup from a doctor, with whom we work closely, that she and the baby are in good health. We don't know the sex of the child."

"What do we say to her?" Dan asked.

"I'll lead the discussion. You just answer the questions she or I ask," Durand said. "Are you ready?"

"Guess so," Dan said as he leaned over to push Eric's hair out of his eyes.

"I'll take you to my office, then bring Tanya in there."

We arranged ourselves on the black leather couch in Durand's office. Nick and Eric huddled close to Dan.

Our attorney entered the office and sat down in a black leather swivel desk chair that had been pulled over to the couch for the meeting. A short woman with long brown hair sat in the tan wing chair that seemed to swallow her up. Her eyes were focused on the floor, except for quick glances at us. She was just barely showing her pregnancy, Durand made the introductions, then asked Tanya to explain why she was putting her child up for adoption.

"I can't support myself, let alone a child," she said. "I have two boys, so I know how much work a baby is. After I got divorced, I had my boys, but I couldn't take the right care of them. I gave them to their father because they'd be better off with him. I just want more for this child than what me or my sisters and brothers got."

"Is money the only problem, Tanya?" Durand asked. "We can refer you to social service agencies."

"No, I can't bring up a child. I still don't know what I'm about, myself. I need to find out who I am and how I fit into the world before I can take on anyone else."

"How do you know the father doesn't want the child?"

"I'm not proud of this, but he's married, and has his own family. He came over to my apartment all the time for about four months. As soon as I told him I was pregnant, he didn't want to see me anymore. He wanted me to have an abortion."

"Did you consider having an abortion?"

"I couldn't do that. I figure it was better to have the child but I didn't ever think I could keep the baby. I just can't deal with it."

"Have you been drunk or used drugs since you became pregnant?"

"I did have some beer when I was pregnant but didn't know I was. Since I found out, I quit drinking. I never did drugs. I do smoke, but I cut way back. I'm down to five cigarettes a day."

"Now let me ask the family some questions. Why do you want to adopt a baby?"

"My daughters were killed last year in an airplane crash," I said, tears forming in my eyes. "I would like the opportunity to bring up more children. I had a hysterectomy, so I can't have any more myself. I would love a baby with all my heart and soul."

"Does the sex of the baby matter?" Durand asked.

"No, you don't get to choose when you have one yourself. We'd love either a girl or a boy."

"Dan, tell Tanya a little about your family."

"Well, we live in Phoenix and like the outdoor life. We have a pool and do a lot of swimming. Both boys play on baseball and basketball teams. We go fishing and camping. I do a lot of golfing and the kids ride along with me. I'm not sure what else to say."

"What do you do for a living?"

"I have a small business and Annie just got an assistant principal job. We plan to have a babysitter come into our house."

"What religion will the baby be?"

"I'm Jewish and Dan's Protestant," I said. "I would like to raise the baby Jewish if the birth mother has no objection."

"It don't matter to me," Tanya said, "as long as the child is raised with religion. I think that's important."

"I do too," I said.

Tanya and I made eye contact for the first time. We nodded in agreement.

"I have another birth mother and family waiting," Durand said as he got up. "We'll meet back here in an hour. That will give you time to make a decision."

He led us out to the lobby of the offices.

Dan looked at Tanya and said," Would you like to go to lunch with us? I think there's a coffee shop in the lobby of this building."

"Sure," she said.

During lunch, Tanya asked the boys about school and their sports activities. Nick told her all about the new house. Eric told her knock-knock jokes and we heard Tanya's laugh for the first time.

By the time we went back up to the offices, the conversation was free flowing and natural.

Durand ushered us into his office, then took Tanya into the conference room.

I tapped my fingers on my arm and shifted around in my seat on the couch.

"What's the matter with you?" Dan asked.

"I'm just nervous. I want her to pick us."

"Yeah, it's a good situation with the boyfriend not being the father of the baby and the father being married. There also aren't any parents in the situation to try to persuade her to keep the baby."

Durand opened the door and sat down.

"You've had a chance to talk with Tanya. What's your decision?"

"If she'll have us, we'll have her," Dan said.

Durand smiled. "Then it's a match," he said. "Tanya really liked the way you listened to your children at lunch. I don't think she came from the kind of home where children were a priority. The due date is the middle of November."

"That should give us plenty of time to get certified for adoption in Arizona," I said. I was already thinking of where the boxes of Emily and Elizabeth's baby quilts were.

"Yes, you need to do that right away."

Durand stood up and shook hands with Dan and me. Nick stuck out his hand, so he shook it. Durand then offered a hand to Eric, but he put his hand behind his back and moved closer to Dan.

"We'll keep in touch and you'll receive a monthly statement of checks that have been written from your account here. I think Tanya is eligible for MediCal, so our office will help her apply for it."

"Thank you for all your help, Durand," I managed to say through the emotion caught in my throat.

As we were riding down in the elevator, I hugged Dan, Nick, and Eric.

"I can't believe this is happening so soon!"

"It's a good thing, we're not getting any younger. We're going to be sixty-two when this baby graduates from college," Dan said, "just in time for us to retire."

"I am so happy! This ranks right up there when I found out I was pregnant with Emily!"

"Can we get ice cream before we get on the plane?" Eric asked.

"Definitely!" I said. "This calls for a celebration with sundaes!"

*　*　*

Dan and I entered the small tan stucco building and almost ran into the receptionist's small desk.

"We have a four o'clock appointment with Collin Webb," Dan told the receptionist.

"Have a seat, I'll tell him you're here."

I sat down on a brown and beige striped love seat. Dan sat in a chair next to me.

"Quite a contrast to Durand's law offices," I said as I surveyed the waiting area.

"Maybe he won't charge us too much," Dan said.

A short, blond, young man with a dark tan came out to greet us.

"He looks too young to be an attorney," Dan whispered.

"That probably says more about our age than his," I whispered back.

Collin Webb's office was small and his huge desk dwarfed him. He sat behind it, put his hands behind his head, and his feet up on his desk.

"Now, what can I do for you?"

"We've arranged with a California attorney to adopt a baby," Dan said. "The baby is due in mid-November. We'd like you to handle the Arizona part of the adoption."

"Why did you go to California to look for a baby? I can give you referrals to Phoenix attorneys."

"I did look into some situations in Phoenix but I wasn't comfortable with their information," I said. "Arizona is also a small place. I'd hate to meet the birth mother in the K mart."

"Well, I've worked closely with the Southwest Adoption Center. I'm on the board of their nonprofit foundation."

"As I said, I wasn't comfortable with their information and their fees," I could hear my voice get the stern teacher edge to it. "I really think you should look into an Arizona adoption." Dan cut the attorney off. "I don't think you understand. The arrangements have already been made! The baby is due in five months. Are you willing to handle the paperwork that needs to be done in Arizona?"

"I can do that for you," Collin said. He curtly turned his chair around and opened the credenza, extracting a packet of papers. "The top page is a representation agreement and my fee. You need to fill out the rest of the packet and send it back as soon as possible."

Dan's eyes narrowed as he read. He passed the top sheet to me. I took a sharp, deep breath when I saw the fee of two thousand dollars. That was close to the fee that the California lawyer was charging for his part of the deal, which was much more involved.

"You'll need to give me a copy of your adoption certification from the county."

"We're still working on that," I said.

"You absolutely have to have it before the baby can be brought back to Arizona," Collin Webb said.

"Is there anything else?" Dan asked.

"No. As soon as you've completed those papers, drop them off with a check so I can get started on this."

The attorney got up and shook only Dan's hand over his desk. After we'd left the building, I turned to Dan and said, "I don't like him very much. He gives me the creeps."

"I don't like him either," Dan said, "But I don't think there's much to the Arizona side of it. He's a prick but he was recommended because he knows people and can get the job done."

*   *   *

June 17, 1987

Dear Emily,

Your birthday's today, and Elizabeth's is on July 1.

I went to visit your grave today. I brought tiny pink roses

and two hundred dollar bills. Why hasn't the grass grown over your graves?

Your joint gravestone will be laid August 16, the anniversary of your deaths. I can find you easily because your Daddy's marker was laid right after the funeral.

I ripped up the bills into small pieces and sprinkled them over your graves. I want you, Emily and Elizabeth. The settlement money is not important, no measure of your worth. I love you today and forever. I'll always miss you.

My tears dripped onto the encrusted dirt, big splats of water like the first drops of a thunderstorm.

I keep the tempest inside, Emily. Sometimes I feel I'm betraying you just by living.

You'd be proud of me. I got a job as an assistant principal. And you're going to have a brother or sister soon. I'm going on the fast track to a new life. I just wish you were here to share it.

Emily and Elizabeth, you're with me in my heart, always, my angels.

Love,
Mommy

*   *   *

I called Susan when she got home from vacation.

"Hi there," Susan said.

"Exciting news, Susan. While you were on vacation, we met with the adoption attorney and a birth mother in Los Angeles. Our baby is going to be born in mid November!"

"What? I can't believe it's all happening so soon!"

"I know. I think they gave us special treatment or it's a slow time for adoption."

"Do you know if the baby is a girl or a boy?"

"No, we won't know until her next checkup in a few weeks. You know they only give Tanya, she's the birth mother, one hundred and fifty dollars for clothes. That doesn't buy much of anything these days. I'm thinking about going over to L A., just for the day, and taking her shopping. That way I can also check out where the hospital is. Wanna come?"

"I'd love to! When are you going?"

"August 1 Nick and Eric are going to Missouri to spend three weeks with their grandparents. It drives me crazy that they're flying there, and alone, but I can't stop their lives because of my fears. I start my new job the third week of August. How does sometime during the first two weeks of August sound? I thought I'd stay with you a few days and play on the beach."

"Perfecto. Vanessa loved the swimsuit and clothes you sent. You are so sweet and too generous. The package came right before we left on vacation. She loved and wore everything in Hawaii."

"I found myself in the girls' department and thinking about my girls' birthdays. I was so sad that I wasn't buying summer clothes for Emily and Elizabeth. It really helped to buy the cute outfits for Vanessa."

"I can hear the strain in your voice. How are you doing, my dear?"

"Everyday I survive a little better. The baby helps a lot although I hate the waiting as much as when I was pregnant myself. I'm still very paranoid that something is going to happen to Dan, Nick, or Eric. If anything happened to Dan, the boys would go back to their mother, and I'd lose my family again. That would be the end of me. That's one of the selfish reasons I want a baby."

"You're a great mother, that's why you should adopt a baby. I'm so happy for you!"

"I gotta go to pick up Eric from his basketball camp. See you in August!"

*   *   *

"She seems very nice," Susan said to me as we waited outside the Nordstom's dressing room while Tanya tried on maternity clothes. "In fact she's so nice it's hard to understand why she wants to give up the baby."

"I know. My stereotype of a birth mother is blown away. She speaks well and has a GED, but she's not working," I said. "It's hard for me to imagine myself in such a position: no family support, no friends, just a boyfriend."

"I remember how freaked out I was in Berkeley when I found out Bruce was having an affair. I had no one, but I had a job and got myself a place to live in a hurry. But she's brave to have this baby and put it up for adoption."

I gave Susan a hug. "I'm certainly grateful that Tanya has made this choice. During lunch I thought I'd ask her about her work experience and help her do a resume."

"Annie, I don't think she's going to find a great job when she's six months pregnant."

"She could use the resume later . . . . "

"You're a hopeless idealist," Susan said as she sighed.

Tanya emerged from the dressing room in her own clothes.

"I liked these two pair of shorts and this pair of jeans. These tops are nice, but if it's too much I'd rather have the pants."

"It's not too much," I said gathering up all the clothes. "We'll take these and I think we should find another two pairs of these jeans. I lived in maternity jeans when I was pregnant."

I found two more pairs of jeans in the same style and size, then paid for the clothes.

"We have plenty of time for lunch. Is that okay with you, Tanya?"

"Sure," she said.

"What kind of food do you want?"

"Anything is okay with me."

As we were being seated in a family restaurant, Tanya said, "Your baby just kicked me. Wanna feel it?"

"I'd love to," I said. I gently put my hand on Tanya's blue blouse where it bulged. Tanya took my hand and directed it to a spot. When I felt the movement my heart soared with a joy I hadn't felt in nearly a year. New life.

"Are you disappointed it's a boy?" Tanya asked.

"No," I said softly. "This baby will have a life of its own. If it was a girl, I'd be comparing her to Emily and Elizabeth."

"Have you decided on a name for the baby?" Tanya asked. "I'd like to have something to call him."

"Dan and I spent a whole weekend on our boat, looking through a book of baby names. I would have loved to call him 'Benjamin,' after my dad who died last October, but my brother had a child last month and named him 'Benjamin.'

"Dan and I had a fun time, trying on all the names. We're going to call him 'Max', after my favorite character in a picture book called *Where the Wild Things Are*. His legal name will be 'Maxwell'."

"Maxwell. I like that name," Tanya said, "It sounds solid."

There was no more conversation, so we opened their menus.

After we had ordered, I said, "Tanya, I'd like you to tell me as much about yourself and Max's father as you are comfortable."

"Okay. I'm short but his father is six feet three inches tall and has black hair. He's very handsome and there's something about him that's almost magnetic. It's hard not to come under his spell. I don't mean that in a bad way, just that he's very persuasive. There's a special word for it."

"Charisma?" Susan offered.

"Yeah, that's it, charisma. He has two children and they're good at school and the older one plays the piano very well. My sons do well at school, and they're both in the band."

"Tanya, I like our arrangement for no contact between you and the baby after he's born. But would you be willing to be found by him after he's an adult?"

It was quiet at the table. After what seemed like an hour but was only a minute or so, Tanya said, "Yes, I would see him. I have a favor to ask you, Annie. Would you send me a letter every year on his birthday, and include a picture?"

"Yes, I'd be glad to do that."

"I just want to know that he's okay."

Our food arrived and we ate in silence.

We drove Tanya back to her apartment, then went looking for the hospital where the baby would be born. My baby, Max.

Susan and I had just enough time to head to the beach. We walked on the sand at the water's edge, close enough to allow the waves to lick our feet.

"Susan, did you notice that Tanya called the baby 'Max' after I told her what his name would be?"

"Yeah, I think that's a good sign that she isn't going to change her mind."

"I worry about that. I'm also worried because the county still hasn't scheduled a social worker to visit us at home. We have to be certified before the baby is born."

"It will all work out, I just know it will. I had a dream the other night. I know you don't believe in psychic phenomena, but listen to this. You were in my dream, hugging a baby. Your heart was glowing through your shirt. So I know you're going to get this baby."

"I'll accept it as a sign. Hell, I'll accept any positive signs these days!"

A wave came and ambushed our legs, drenching the bottom of our skirts. We laughed so hard, we almost fell over.

*   *   *

CHAPTER 21

The leaves like Women interchange
Exclusive Confidence—
Somewhat of nods and somewhat
Portentous inference.

-Emily Dickinson

Click. I recognized the feeling after five minutes of talking to my new boss, Joanne Johnson. We were sitting in Jo's office, talking about what I would be doing as assistant principal, when I realized that we were on the same brain waves, just as I was with Susan.

"And you'll be in charge of the special area teachers, all special projects, and liaison with the parent groups. This week I want you to get settled in your office and work on the class lists. You need to delete the students for whom we've received requests for records and add the new registrants. Let me know if the first grade classes get over 29 students."

"We won't ever have time for lunch once the school year starts," she said, "so let's plan to eat out every day this week, if that's okay with you."

"It sounds fine."

"I'll call a few of the principals to go with us so you can meet them."

"Thanks, I appreciate that."

I went back to my office. This is another chapter of my new life, I thought. My own office, small, but my own. The large green metal desk took up most of the floor space. The filing cabinet was empty. The child's roll top desk and a pie cupboard, both of which I found when antiquing, were my attempts to make the office homey. I'm a nester, no doubt about it. I placed a framed family portrait, taken for the adoption applications, on my desk, then put a smaller frame with a picture of Emily and Elizabeth next to it.

Tomorrow it would be a year since the crash. In keeping with the Jewish tradition, the unveiling of the gravestone was on Sunday, a year after their deaths. My mother and sister and Susan were flying in for it. I hadn't been out to the cemetery since the girls' birthdays. I shook my head, in a physical effort to clear my head of these thoughts, and went out to see the secretary about getting some file folders, pens and pencils.

* * *

I heard the drone of the rabbi's voice but I stared at the long stone that went over the graves of both of my daughters. Susan had done the sketch of a sun and a rainbow, our pet names for Emily and Elizabeth. The stonecutter etched it faithfully on a gray slice of granite. The sun had a smile on its face; the rainbow was trying to catch everyone's attention. How like Emily and Elizabeth!

The stone had their names, their birth and death dates and a quotation from a Sara Teasdale poem, "Children's faces looking up, holding wonder like a cup."

It was still hard to associate these graves with my two spirited children. I still somehow expected them to come around the corner and wonder what the fuss was about. The tears didn't flow freely until the makeshift morgue flashed inside my head, and the reality that Emily and Elizabeth would never be back.

Dan was standing next to me with Nick and Eric on his other side. I peeked over at them and wondered how much they understood. Sometimes they talked about memories of Emily and Elizabeth, but never their deaths.

My sister and mother were quietly crying nearby. Carol and Susan were standing by the rabbi, holding each other's hands.

The talking stopped. The rabbi came up and said something to me, I wasn't sure what. Dan took my arm and led me back to his car. I got in and we rode in silence back to the house.

When we got back to our new house, I was surprised to see more people. Elissa had brought over cold cuts and was setting up a buffet. Had these people been at the cemetery? Please God, I prayed, I don't want to slide back down that tunnel of depression. Give me the strength to at least repress things.

I put on my public mask before I got into the house. I was aloof from everyone, politely accepting condolences, not listening to the comments.

Later in the afternoon Dan took my mother, sister, and Susan to the airport to catch their planes. I went up to my room, threw myself on the bed, and heaved sobs with no tears.

A portrait of "the friends" after the unveiling of the gravestone. Back row, left to right: Susan G., Marcy, Annie, Susan B. Karlene, and Carol Front row, left to right: Elissa, Eric, Veronica

*   *   *

I turned over in bed and looked at the clock for what seemed like the hundredth time. It was finally five o'clock, not too ridiculously early to get up for the first day of school. I shut off the alarm, set for six, and went into the bathroom to take my shower, grateful to have my life.

I carefully applied my eye makeup as if that could help make the day go well. I put the toilet lid down and sat on it to put on my stockings so I wouldn't have to do it on the bed and wake up Dan. After putting on the carefully chosen beige raw silk skirt and blouse and the low taupe heels, I looked in the full length mirror on the back of the bathroom door. I looked professional. The outfit was also cool enough to help me battle the warm temperatures. It would be over ninety degrees in the shade this morning when I directed parents and students to their classrooms.

I said a silent prayer that I hadn't made some big mistake and didn't know enough to recognize it.

On the way out of the bedroom I gently touched Dan's shoulder and whispered, "It's early, almost six. I'm going to make some tea, then go to school."

"Good luck," Dan said.

I kissed his cheek.

On the way to school I stopped at a donut shop and picked up a dozen chocolate covered donuts for the office staff. When I arrived at school at six-thirty, ten cars were already in the parking lot. I knew that Jo would be there.

"Are you ready for the thundering masses?" she asked as I stepped into the office.

"I think so."

"Most of the parents came down over the weekend to check the posted class lists. There will be a line of parents trying to change their child's teacher. Stand firm. We won't change the classes. We met all of the written parent requests."

At seven-thirty I went out to greet parents and students as they arrived on campus. There were many volunteer parents who helped the children off the buses, directed students to the right rooms, figured out bus schedules, and wrote bus tags.

Although I knew that the school was ninety-five percent white, I still wasn't prepared for it. How would I learn to tell all these blondes apart when they were wearing the same cute outfits?

At lunchtime, the cafeteria was a nightmare. The line was backed up with at least five classes waiting. The map I had so carefully drawn for the table seating didn't work because there was such a back up in the line. One mother who came to have lunch with her child said she had to go back to work before she was even served any food. The woman's makeup melted from the heat and ran unattractively in rivulets down her face.

"I hope you get this better organized!" she snapped at me as she left.

The most confusion was at dismissal. Parents refused to move cars that blocked the path of the buses. Although the younger children wore bus tags, several got on the wrong bus. One of the buses was twenty minutes late. I was so hot and sweaty I thought I would liquefy into the sidewalk.

By four-thirty all the students were safely home, as far as the office knew. Jo and I sat across from each other in Jo's office.

"Welcome to administration! The school year is off and running!" she said. "So what do you think?"

"It certainly wasn't boring," I replied. "Most of the parents were very nice and helped so much. Then there were a few . . . "

"Yeah, who is Mrs. Hays? I have a message from the superintendent to call about her daughter."

"She was pretty rude, but I was polite. She's mad because I wouldn't change her daughter's class. The mom wants the kid to be in the same class as her friends."

"Almost all of the parents who requested a change will call you tomorrow and say that their child likes the class he or she was assigned."

"Mrs. Hays didn't let Jennifer start school. She said she's keeping her out until she gets in the right class."

"Then she's going to be a problem. The superintendent will probably ask me to grant her request for a class change."

"Are you going to do it?"

"I hate to give in, but if he asks me to, I will. It's all part of the game. You save your stands for bigger issues. I have a few phone calls to make. Why don't you go home? It's been a hot and hard day. You don't have to stay as late as I do. I do it out of choice. I also don't have a big family at home."

"I just want to straighten my desk before I leave," I said.

I went back to my office, put things in piles so it wouldn't look so messy, and drove to Eric's school to pick him up from after school care. His school had started the day before mine. When he saw me he jumped up, ran and hugged me.

"Let's go, I don't like it here."

"What's the matter?"

"It's boring and I don't have any friends."

"Do you want me to talk to the people in charge?"

"No!"

"You know Eric, after we get our baby, there will be a babysitter at home. Would you rather come home after school then?"

"Yes! Can't I stay at home now with Nick?"

"No, he's only ten. That's too young to look after you. Is anyone bothering or hurting you?"

"No, I just don't have any friends here."

"You'll make some. It's only the second day of school. We'll talk about it at home."

I signed him out, feeling the guilt familiar to working mothers.

*   *   *

The thin woman left the steam room, leaving Carol and me alone.

"I thought that old lady would never leave!" Carol said. "Tell me what's going on in your life. We never get a chance to talk. What's up with the adoption?"

"Everything's on track. The county social worker came for the home visit. I told her about the tricky timing, but she said she couldn't promise when the certification would go through. She did say that we passed inspection. The paperwork and the judge's okay is all that's left. Eric was so weird about the visit. We had told his teacher he would be late that day, but he had a substitute. He told me when she asked why he was late, he said 'Personal business.'"

"How's the birth mother?"

"I called California and the adoption attorney's secretary told me that the latest report from Tanya's doctor says she's still healthy and due on November 15."

"When do you actually get the baby?"

"The California attorney's office will call me when Tanya goes into labor. I'll take the first flight out and go to the hospital. Tanya had said I could be in the delivery room, but I decided not to do that. I should see the baby as soon as he goes up to the nursery. Susan is going to meet me at the hospital. Dan and the boys will fly over the next day. We'll stay a few days, then come home. I can't wait!"

"The baby's room looks so cute with all that bunny stuff. I want to have a baby shower for you but I'll wait until you're back in Phoenix before we pick the date. How much time are you taking off work?"

"I was scared to tell Jo, my principal, about the baby. When I finally did, she was great and approved a two week leave. I'm going to advertise for a babysitter at the end of October so I'll have someone hired before the baby is born."

"How's your new job?"

"It's only been two months, but my old library seems years ago. Life is much more hectic than when I was a teacher. There's always something going on. This week a third grader was sent to the office because he brought a baggie with powdered sugar to school and was sniffing it like cocaine during recess."

"You're kidding!"

"No, I talked with him in my office about the meaning of a drug free environment and the wrong decision he had made to bring the sugar to school and use it that way. He cried a little. I gave him a detention and sent him back to class. About thirty minutes later I went to his classroom and delivered a 'drug speech' to the whole class. Then I went back to the office and called the student's mother and told her what happened."

"Was she embarrassed?"

"That was the weird part. She was upset with me! She knew that he had brought the powdered sugar to school because he had told her it was for a science experiment. She seemed totally unconcerned that her son had lied to her. She thought the faked cocaine sniffing was funny, and I should have taken it as a harmless joke."

"He's probably imitating her."

"Could be. Anyway, another thirty minutes went by and I got another phone call, this time from the student's father, who's an attorney. He thought I should apologize to his son for humiliating him in front of his peers."

"No!"

"Yes! I explained to the dad that in no way did I pinpoint him or the incident when speaking with the class. He demanded a meeting the following morning with the principal. That's the good part about being an assistant principal, the really irate parents insist on speaking to the principal."

"What happened in the meeting?"

"I wasn't included, but the principal did back me up and smooth the parents' ruffled feathers. Anyway, I can tell this is going to get harder with a baby. I'll just have to wait and see how it goes after that. It's too hot in here. I'm dying! Time to get out."

"Okay. Are you up for lunch?"

"I could go for a salad."

I ran out of the steam room to a sink in the locker area. I turned on the cold water and splashed some on my face. When I looked in the mirror, I was horrified to see that my face was so red it was almost purple.

"I definitely cooked for too long this time, Carol. I'm going to have to drink a gallon of water to recover."

"But your skin will look beautiful once it goes back to your natural color," Carol said as she got in the shower.

*   *   *

CHAPTER 22

Contained in this short Life
Are magical extents

-Emily Dickinson

The expressions on the second graders' faces reflected boredom with the phonics lesson. I was observing Mrs. Franklin's teaching and composing a gentle note that contained a strong suggestion on alternative strategies. I flipped the notebook page and made a fourth attempt at the note.

An all call announcement sent me back to the office before I completed my task.

"It's a long distance call for you," the secretary said.

I went into my office and shut the door before picking up the phone.

"Annie Weissman speaking, how may I help you?"

"Hi, this is Marcia, from Durand Cook's office. Your birth mother, Tanya, is in labor at the hospital and it's going well."

"Oh my God! Thanks so much, I'll get on a plane as soon as I can!"

"You'll need to call our office tomorrow."

"Oh yeah, sure."

My heart was hammering, my adrenaline was spiking. I hung up and immediately called Susan to arrange a rendezvous at the L.A. airport.

*　　*　　*

Susan and I walked into the hospital hand in hand. The hospital itself looked like a motel onto which rooms had been added every few years.

"I'm glad we found this place last time we were here. I'm so excited I was a menace on the road," Susan said.

"I know, it was a white knuckle ride for me," I said.

We asked the woman in the pink volunteer's uniform in patient information about Tanya and were sent down to the labor and delivery nurse's station. I asked the nurse the status of Tanya's delivery. The nurse disappeared. A few minutes later she reappeared bearing the news that the baby was leaving the delivery room for the nursery.

After asking directions, we ran down the green speckled floors of the hallways to the glass walled nursery. I went up to the door.

"I'm the adoptive mother of Tanya Hammer's baby," I said to the young nurse. "My name is Annie Weissman and this is the godmother. May we see him?"

"He's just arrived and has to stay under the lights for at least an hour before you can hold him. Would you like to come in and see him?"

"Oh yes!"

"For the protection of all of the babies you need to put on the hospital greens, including the shoe covers."

We donned the outfits over our clothes.

"You look very good as a doctor," I said to Susan. "Ever thought of going to medical school?"

"Yeah, right!" was the reply.

The nurse led us to a plastic crib on wheels with heat lamps above it.

I looked at the pink ball of clay who was letting out fierce howls. It was love at first sight. He's protesting his naked state, I thought.

"I was just about to wash him," the nurse said. She picked the baby up with professional confidence and took him over to a stainless steel sink. She scrubbed him, with soap, including the dark hair that was stuck to his head in swirls. She toweled him off, all the while ignoring the cries that were piercing my heart. The nurse laid him, still unclothed, back in the crib. The crying did not abate. The baby's arms and legs were off the mattress, tensed in anger. His face looked like one big open mouth.

I listened as his cries reach a crescendo. When I could no longer endure it, I asked the nurse, "Isn't it bad for him to get so upset?"

"No, it helps to warm his body and get the circulation going. Crying is just a baby's form of exercise."

"This is the part that I never saw when I gave birth," I whispered under my breath to Susan. "Do you remember being in the recovery room with nurses kneading your stomach while they whisked the baby away to the nursery for tests?"

"That part was sort of hazy for me," Susan said.

Susan and I stood as sentinels over the baby's crib for an hour that seemed to stretch on for days. Finally the nurse came over and put a diaper, a hospital tee shirt, and a blue and white striped knitted stocking cap on him. She swaddled the still yowling infant in a white cotton blanket and turned to me.

"Do you want to hold him?"

"Oh, yes!"

I took the precious package into my arms and pressed the baby to my heart. I walked slowly around the small room, humming a tune I remembered my father singing to me, 'Too-ra-loo-ra-loora-too-ra-loora lie." The baby quieted.

I sat down in a rocking chair and leaned over to whisper in the baby's ear, "Max, I've been waiting impatiently for your arrival. You are everything I wanted. I'm your momma and I love you."

I sat back and rocked, drinking in the wonder of my new baby. His closed eyelids were puffy and pink pieces. Although his body was hidden from me, he relaxed in the cloth cocoon. I felt a peace and joy I hadn't known for over a year. Here was a new beginning, another reason to get out of bed in the morning. I said a silent "Thank you" to God.

I lost track of time. I looked up and saw Susan sitting across from me, smiling.

"It's your turn, godmother. I've got to call Dan and the boys."

Susan took the baby in her arms and sat in the rocking chair. She, too, whispered in the baby's ear.

*   *   *

The next morning Susan and I went back to the airport to pick up Dan, Nick, and Eric. I was feeling an odd mixture of excitement, exhaustion, and fear. I was always afraid when any one I loved was flying. My husband and two sons arrived safe and sound an hour later. We all drove straight to the hospital.

Nick and Eric took turns holding and feeding Max. I could feel the emotions, kept on ice for a year, thawing when I saw the gentle and loving way that my menfolk took to this baby. I knew he was accepted as one of the tribe.

Later in the morning, we drove to the attorney's office to check on the paperwork. Durand was out, but the secretary asked me if I minded taking over the Arizona disclosure questionnaire and helping Tanya fill it out. It had just arrived from the Arizona attorney.

We rushed back to the hospital, just in time to see Tanya, who was ready to check out.

"You've been here less than twenty-four hours!" I said.

"I know, but my part is done. I did take one look at Max through the glass. You've got a beautiful baby."

"And I thank you for making it possible. Before you go, will you help me fill out some background questions that need to be done for Arizona?"

"Okay, if it doesn't take long. My boyfriend is going to be here soon."

We went through the questions, with me writing down the responses. Tanya couldn't answer some of the ones that related to Max's father. We rushed through the last few as Tanya's boyfriend stood at the door of her room, tapping his foot. I gave Tanya a hug and wished her well.

I went back to the nursery and watched through the glass as Nick fed Max. My heart swelled, proving right the old adage "there's always room for one more." I saw Dan carefully put the baby in his crib when he fell asleep.

When we went back to Susan's house, Dan and the boys went to the beach while I slept. After dinner we went back to the hospital to visit Max.

The next morning we spent time with Max then drove to the attorney's office to check on the timetable of when we could go back to Phoenix. There was a short wait until he could see us. Durand Cook's grim expression gave me a knot in my stomach.

"Here's the Arizona background questionnaire," I said. "Tanya answered as many questions as she could."

"When can we go back to Phoenix?" Dan asked.

"There's a problem, a big problem," Durand said slowly.

"Oh God, has Tanya changed her mind?" I asked.

"No, the problem is in Arizona. Tanya still has an appointment to sign her rights away tomorrow morning. It's three days according to Arizona law. No, the problem is with your Arizona attorney. He has informed me that the judge will hold up your adoption certification so you can't adopt this baby because you paid the living expenses of the mother, which is against Arizona law."

"That's ridiculous! He knew about that from the beginning! What we did was legal in California!" Dan thundered. "What needs to be done?"

"I'm not sure anything can be done, at least that's what he's telling me."

"Max is our brother!" Nick said.

I looked at my family, caught in another web of tragedy.

"Max is our baby!" I said before retreating inside myself, hearing but unable to respond, just like last year, after the crash.

"We'll put you at the top of the list for a baby whose mother doesn't need you to pay her living expenses," the attorney said.

"I don't think you understand," Dan said. "He is our baby. Your job is to figure out how we get him back to Arizona. I don't care what you have to do, my family will not give him up!"

"I'll call your attorney again. He mentioned that the county attorney was thinking about using you as an example to cut off out of state adoptions."

I broke through the box I had built around myself. I was going to fight for Max.

"You just tell that son of a bitch that I'll go straight to the news media. They'll jump at a story about the county attorney taking away a baby from a woman whose children were killed in an airplane crash. It's not good publicity for a reelection campaign."

Durand Cook reached out and held my hand. "I'll go back to my office and try some ball busting."

* * *

CHAPTER 23

The Sun and Fog contested
The Government of Day—
The Sun took down his Yellow Whip
And drove the Fog away—

-Emily Dickinson

Tears silently streamed down my face. Dan got out of his chair and stood behind me, with his hands on my shoulders.

"What's going to happen, Daddy?" Eric asked.

"We may have to stay an extra few days, that's all. Max is our baby and we'll take him home."

The wait seemed interminable. I closed my eyes. I imagined Dan in a bloody, fatal car accident and Nick and Eric packing their things to live with their mother. It seemed so real I jumped when Dan's hand kneaded my shoulder. I opened my eyes and my mouth fluttered a smile when I saw Nick and Eric, fidgeting and impatient with the slowness of adult business.

Finally Durand came back, still with his grim expression.

His tie was askew and his white shirt needed to be tucked further into his gray linen pants.

"I need some information from you. Did you notice anything unusual about your conversations with your attorney, Collin Webb?"

"As a matter of fact, yes," Dan said. "He wanted us to adopt in Arizona. We told him that the arrangements had been made with your office, but he kept at us about it. Annie explained how she was not impressed with the adoption agency in town he recommended."

"I think this has more to do with a power and money struggle between California and Arizona attorneys than with you personally. Do you know if Collin Webb has the ear of the judge in this case?"

"We hired him because we heard he knew his way around adoptions and the judges that oversee the process."

Durand Cook's expression changed. His lips pursed, his body leaned forward, like a panther stalking prey.

"Okay, that gives an insight into his behavior. All is not lost. I'm not going to let them use you as a martyr for their greed. I can do this, but it won't be finished today."

"We were going to take the baby from the hospital today."

"Call the nursery and tell them you're too tired today, that you will pick up the baby tomorrow. Do not tell them there's any trouble. We don't want to involve any social service agency."

I came to life. Hope spread and woke my mind, body, and soul. A veil of uncertainty still lingered.

"I'll call you when I know something definite. Hopefully this evening, but maybe not until tomorrow morning."

Dan stood and shook the attorney's hand.

"I knew we could trust you," he said.

I rose slowly from my seat, walked to Durand, took his hand in both of mine, and squeezed it.

"Thank you for saving my life," I said.

Dan put his arm around me as we walked out.

*   *   *

I waited by the phone at Susan's, feeling its presence even as we ate Susan's luscious pasta dinner.

After dinner I watched T.V. to distract myself from the current crisis. It didn't work. Susan sat next to me and held my hand.

"Why did things turn to shit when they were going so well?" I asked. "Max is my baby and I can't face losing him. The saw-toothed monster that's been chewing on my heart for over a year was beaten back when I held Max close and sang to him. I'm afraid the monster will consume me if Max were to disappear from my life."

I lifted my feet to the seat of my chair, put my arms around my knees, and hugged them.

Susan hugged me harder.

Durand Cook finally called.

"Do you have any good news?"

"Yes, I do. I thought California had a crazy legal system, but Arizona is much worse. When I realized it was an ego problem, not a legal problem, I did some fast talking and came up with a deal. My office needs to reimburse you for the living expenses of the mother and I agreed to forego my fee. In exchange the judge will sign your certification as an adoptive family and you can bring the baby back to Arizona. It will still be a few days to clear up the paperwork, but it will work out if you have someone in California who can reimburse my office for the living expenses of the birth mother."

"That's not a problem. She can also cover your fee."

"Ethically I can't discuss that."

I started to speak, but emotion closed my throat. I took a deep breath and said, "I understand and truly appreciate the nature of what you have done. There'll be a place reserved in heaven for you."

"I think the motivation on the part of Collin Webb and the Arizona judge was to try to stop the rising tide of out-of-state attorneys receiving the fees for adoptions. That stinks!"

"I'm just glad you could fix it for us. What happens now with Max?"

"The birth mother will be coming in tomorrow afternoon to sign the paper that severs her rights. I'll call the hospital when she does and you can take Max from the hospital. You need to stay in California until I give you a check for the money spent on Tanya's living expenses, the accounting, and documentation."

"How long will that take?"

"You'll probably be ready to leave on Monday."

"Does Dan have to sign anything? He needs to get back to work and the boys would like to get back home for their basketball games."

"They can go home. Your signature will be fine."

"Thanks again, Durand, you literally saved my life," I said as I ended our conversation.

"Yes! Thank you God!" I shouted as I collapsed on the couch. Tears flowed freely and sobs unclogged my throat.

As soon as I caught my breath, I sat up and yelled for everyone to hear, "Max is ours!"

They all came bounding in, shouting joyously.

"Can we go and pick him up now?" Eric asked.

"No, we need to wait until tomorrow, until Tanya has signed the adoption papers."

"He's our baby!" yelled Nick as he jumped up for a hug from Dan.

Dan looked over Nick's head and nodded at me. Susan leaned over and hugged me. Then everyone was hugging.

"Boys, please play outside for a while," I said.

I told the adults the financial situation. Susan said it was no problem for her to write a check for expenses.

"Could you also manage $2500 in cash?" I asked. "I'll send you a check as soon as I get home."

"Don't reimburse me," Susan said. "It's too obvious and might endanger the legal proceedings. After the adoption is final, we'll talk about paying me back for the living expenses and the 'gift' for Durand."

"But it might be $10,000! That's a lot of money!"

"I know, but it's a terrific investment in my godson. I don't need the money right now and Max does. I'm just glad I can help you out for a change. End of discussion."

The depth of our friendship could never be mined.

*　　*　　*

I drove Dan and the boys back to the airport early the next morning. At the curb, I hugged each son, despite protests of outward displays of affection from Nick.

Dan gave me a bear hug and said, "We'll see you soon in Phoenix."

I drove away from the airport, my anxieties running rampant as I knew they were boarding the plane. Before returning to Susan's, I stopped at a convenience mart to buy a Hershey's bar, a Clark bar and a Milky Way. I finished two of them in the car.

*   *   *

Susan went to the bank for the cash for the attorney's "gift" while I went to a supermarket and bought supplies for the baby: distilled water, baby formula, and diapers. When I went back to her house I unpacked the baby blankets and clothes I had brought from home. I smoothed the cross-stitch outfit I had embroidered for Max to wear home from the hospital, and put it in the diaper bag.

When Susan got home, we belted the car seat in securely, and headed straight to the hospital.

Max was there in his crib, waiting for me. He was so sweet, easily satisfied with a bottle, a change of diapers, or a song while I rocked him.

I cooed and rocked and loved what was almost lost to me.

A little after three the nurse told me that the attorney's office had called. I could now take my baby from the hospital. Susan had hugged me and stroked Max's cheek.

"Let's go straight to the attorney's," she said. "I hate to have this cash on me."

"It seems like time stood still for a year and now my life is going a hundred miles an hour: a new house, a new job, a new baby. My new life."

"All will be fine. You deserve a new life," Susan said.

*   *   *

Max was asleep when we got to the attorney's office so I stayed with him in the parked car in the building's garage.

Susan went up to the law offices asked the receptionist if Durand Cook's secretary was still around. The secretary brought Susan back to her desk.

"I'm here to pay for the living expenses of Tanya, the birth mother of Anne Weissman and Dan Schroff's baby. Do you have the exact amount owed?"

"Yes, I just finished the accounting."

Susan made out the check and received a receipt. Then she brought out a manila envelope from her oversized purse.

"Please put this in the safe here. It has the instructions on the outside that it is to be given to Durand Cook on December 15. Will you make sure he gets it then?"

"Certainly."

"Annie is in the car with the baby. He's sleeping. When will the papers be ready for her to sign so they can get back to Phoenix?"

"Everything should be ready on Monday. I have it on Mr. Cook's calendar for ten in the morning."

"Thank you, I'll give her that message."

Susan returned to the car and slid in the front seat.

* * *

"The account is paid, my dear, including the 'gift' for Durand Cook."

We hugged each other, then looked in the back seat at the sleeping baby.

"He must be having a good dream," I said. "He's smiling."

"He's dreaming about his new life with the best family in the world," Susan said.

I closed my eyes and envisioned Emily and Elizabeth.

My life closed twice but I opened the door to happiness again.

* * *

November 15, 1988

Dear Emily,

I brought Max home today. I'm sad that you won't know your brother. I can't overlap my two lives.

I haven't gotten over the loss of you and Elizabeth. I

never will. Holidays and birthdays will always be tough. Nothing will ever replace you or the special bond we had. But as one door closes, another opens. I have a second life to enjoy with another family. They deserve a mother who is willing to experience all of life, including happiness.

I'll love you always and forever.

Love,
Mommy

Dan, Nick, Annie, and Eric holding Max.

*   *   *

Made in United States
North Haven, CT
20 January 2024

47688762R00117